Courage to Heal
The way I found to get my life back

I. Leticia Robles García

Norma González Hermoso

María del Rocío Vázquez Escalona

BALBOA.PRESS
A DIVISION OF HAY HOUSE

Balboa Press books may be ordered through booksellers or by contacting:

Balboa Press
A Division of Hay House
1663 Liberty Drive
Bloomington, IN 47403
www.balboapress.com
844-682-1282

Print information available on the last page.

ISBN: 978-1-9822-6857-2 (sc)
ISBN: 978-1-9822-6858-9 (e)

Balboa Press rev. date: 05/24/2022

Index:

PART 3 THE EXIT DOOR

INTRODUCTION

Situations occur throughout life that give us the opportunity to grow as human beings; we establish links with our family and social environment that determine our attitudes and behavior, thus shaping our personality.

Events occur that form our perception of reality, we have moments of happiness that make us feel complete; but we also need to learn to face difficult situations derived from the search for our identity and from the construction of a life project, in which we do not always experience pleasant or satisfactory situations. That is the duality that makes up the human being, a series of contradictory emotions that can take us from joy to sadness or from anger to fear.

Each person will find a different path to achieve personal development within a framework of freedom, which will allow them to regain the stability and self-esteem necessary to build their life.

In this book you may find a story similar to yours, which like many others, will surely make you reflect on your own life. The acquired experience will lead you to understand how to get back on track to recover your life project, how to seek help when it is necessary; because the most important thing to bring about a change is having the ability to realize that it is necessary to rebuild and heal with courage.

Surely you know people who have been brave warriors in the process of healing their emotional wounds.

This book is dedicated to all those people we had the joy of meeting and to those who will come. We hope that these lines serve not only as a reminder but also as a hope for future generations.

The authors of "COURAGE TO HEAL", we combine experiences obtained during more than 15 years in the teaching of courses in the field of psychology and education, related to awareness, self-help and self-knowledge.

We have met heroic students who in our courses have given their whole souls to achieve a change, we are also brave survivors of difficult situations.

This is a book written by a team that has put their whole heart and enthusiasm toward achieving this goal.

In order to combine these experiences, the book is structured in this way:

- A neutral main character: everyone can imagine it with the gender of their choice.

- A story, compiled from our own experiences and others that we have witnessed, where few characters appear, also neutral, the names and cities are fictitious.

- References and tools

ICONOGRAPHY USED

When you have to return to the story:

Small definitions:

Did you know?

Reflections, references and some exercises:

Curious facts:

The authors:

Dedications

I wish with much love to facilitate conscious evolution
to a fuller, lighter and more resilient life.

To my kids and grandkids.

In gratitude: Leticia Robles

For you who are in the process of renewal and personal growth.

Norma González Hermoso

With all my love for you companion, travel companion...

Rocío Vázquez Escalona

Part 1
The Chaos

CHAPTER 1
Awareness and Seeking Help

"Your vision will become clear only when you look into your heart.
Who looks outside, dreams; who looks inside, awakes".
CARL GUSTAV JUNG

AWARENESS

One day I woke up and was still crying, I sat on the bed and said what is happening?

Years go by and I still don't see clearly how to neutralize some family or relationship problems, my children are growing up and I want them to have a different life, one of them is five years old and the other eleven; while I am living a stormy relationship, thinking about how to get out of it.

Also, a family event would be about to change my life, my cousin Tricia, who was very close to me, just died.

It is a difficult moment in my life, it seems that the losses are gathering, she was very young. Tricia was the person who opened the path to spirituality for me, which marked in me a new vision about how to rebuild my life.

How can we achieve this rebuilding process? The first thing is to realize. The ability to *"realize"* (awareness). allows us to integrate, recognize our sensations, emotions and feelings, that is, to be aware of what we think, imagine, remember or anticipate.

I have always thought that there must be something more to life, and it should not be based solely on the typical standards that prevail around us.

In the family I was the most controversial member, I was constantly questioning: Where do I come from? Where do I go? Does God exist? Where is our soul located? Can people heal? Can we move forward or improve? Are there advances in the study of body energy? And can self-destructive thoughts and patterns change before they become

"To realize (awareness). is a concept related to the capacity that we have to identify by ourselves what happens inside us and the world that surrounds us. It helps us to understand more clearly what we feel and want, being the first step to achieve what we really want". (Perls, 1974).

"Fritz Perls (humanistic psychologist), stated that this need to realize is related to self-regulation. Awareness can be curative, we can trust the wisdom of the organism". (Perls, 1974).

"Beliefs are a petrified code of one or more moments lived in the past". (Flèche & Olivier, 2014).

ankylosing beliefs that do us much harm and lead us to self-sabotage?

According to various theories, this situation is related to patterns learned from previous generations; as *Bert Hellinger* would say, "These *beliefs* are the product of the psychic inheritance that is imprinted in the depths of our being, in our genes and in the collective unconscious of our family and have the capacity to be transmitted from generation to generation".

These patterns are generating a series of *introjects* in our personal unconscious and in our collective unconscious. An introject is the product of a psychological process, where a person appropriates ideas, beliefs or attitudes that are not their own, rather they are the result of interaction with other people, so we cannot realize that they exist unconsciously.

Through this process, *beliefs and paradigms* will be generated that can be both positive and negative and that largely generate part of our conflicts.

Beliefs are also the product of the repetition of introjects, family, friends, religious communities, educators, caregivers, society and culture, being transmitted from generation to generation.

In fact, the main limiting belief shapers are family, society, and culture.

It is not about blaming or judging anyone, because most of the people my age come from families with the same educational background, especially in a Latin America, where education is more conventional, closed and everything is questionable by society.

"Bert Hellinger, German philosopher, theologian and pedagogue, creator of the Family Constellations. For him, beliefs formed in the unconscious can prevent behavioral changes and obstruct our path of personal growth". (Hellinger Sciencia, 2019).

"An introject is made up of ideas, concepts, norms and beliefs that acquire from infancy. They are usually acquired by the relationship of people who are significant in our life: parents, grandparents, teachers, etc. It is difficult to identify when ideas or attitudes are not really your own, but are the result of the influence of other people".

"A paradigm is made up of a set of conceptions or beliefs that characterize an era. Normally, they correspond to ideas of a scientific or philosophical nature, but it is also understood as a particular approach or point of view".

At that time I could not imagine and think that all this spiritual dimension that we live in the 21st century would open up. Thank God and the great thinkers of this age!

The first books I read about spirituality, thanks to my cousin Tricia, made me interested in topics such as "Life after life" -before her loss- and then I started reading some classic books such as *Metaphysics 1 and 2* by Cony Méndez, *You can Heal your Life* by Louise Hay, *The power of intention* by *Wayne Dyer* by among others.

And it was there that I began to think about many very deep things, which I now see in a very different and simpler way, however, they were the turning point for me to decide to continue on my path of searching. For the first time I had felt the great power of *"Awareness"* with all its intensity and the abrupt need to find a way out.

Who would say that after a long time and falling in love with the study of the brain and its relationship with the heart. The mixture of all the things that formed me forged a very interesting part in me and in my training, which is called psycho-emotional-spiritual health, and which is now the basis of my system of therapeutic work related with those pillars.

Let's go back then to that origin of stormy relationships. When I was in junior high and high school, I also had some non-investiture partners, because they were rebels, not very committed, and it was the age to "be at the party". I remember that it was fashionable to go to hippie gatherings without many limits in various cities, the Beatles, the Monkeys were popular. People only smoked marijuana or used hallucinogenic mushrooms, *sometimes*

"Wayne W. Dyer was an internationally renowned author and speaker in the fields of self-development and spiritual growth. Over the four decades of his career, he wrote more than 40 books... he overcame many obstacles to make his dreams come true and spent much of his life showing others how to do the same. His main message was that every person has the potential to live an extraordinary life".
https://www.drwaynedyer.com/about-dr-wayne-dyer/

LSD. At that time, there were not as many variety of chemical drugs as amphetamines, heroin, cocaine, etc. Therefore, those of us who did not consume these types of drugs were considered "out of fashion", since I was never interested in using.

I am telling you that I come from a family where most of them are academics in the exact sciences area, imagine what happened when I said that I was going to study a career in the humanist field.

There were years in which I felt that I could not meet family expectations, which made me feel frustration and a bit of rejection, and I also began to show frank *signs of rebellion*, a mask whose only purpose -now I understand was to show the sadness and disapproval that I felt.

The situation is that the years went by and I observed that I was not the only one who had those problems.

I am currently coaching with a mind, energy and spirit approach, and many of my clients have also been immersed in stormy relationships. The difference is that current age, things have changed a lot, people have much more severe addictions, money with just one job is not sufficient, divorces have increased proportionally, and social insecurity is not even mentioned.

More information about the risks of the internet in the Annex

The variety of chemical drugs on the market is scary and dangerous. Not to mention that the number of addictions has also intensified and an important number has been recognized in the area of psychology: from addiction to drugs, alcohol, food, sex, violence, games that generate adrenaline release, cigarettes, food, coffee, nicotine, vapers, pornography, addiction to work, suffering, etc. etc. etc., up to the famous video games, going through a whole range of devices and tools for using the internet.

I clarify, although this time has led us to evolve in communications and computing in a fast and efficient way and has provided us with effective platforms for work, and social networks that support the marketing of businesses, as well as making video calls all over the world; The truth is that there are many problems that have been detected with the misuse of *social networks* and the Internet. At the same time, multiple crimes exist that are committed in the deep web and all the dangers that lead to people who are already more vulnerable such as our adolescents and in particular our children, who live terrible experiences of abuse, usurpations and lies of "scammers" (scammers on *the Internet*). and bullying, which later we will talk about bullying or cyberbullying in Annex 1 of the book.

The worst thing is that most of the people who hide behind a camera and who tell lies surely also have their own history of stormy relationships and soul wounds, so they look for masks to relate in an erroneous way to other human beings.

Yes, we are having a difficult time to live!

TOXIC AND NURTURING RELATIONSHIPS

So when is it time to change?

I remember very well that years ago, in the psychology classes I took, I had a very beloved teacher, who taught us in one semester the difference between nurturing and toxic relationships.

Fritz Perls, A humanistic psychologist, born in 1893 wrote a Gestalt prayer which if we understand it, is a balm for this kind of soul wound:

"I am me, you are you. I do my thing and you do yours.

I am not in this world to meet your expectations, nor are you to meet mine.

I am me, you are you. If at any time or at some point we meet it will be wonderful, if not, it cannot be remedied.

Lacking in love for myself, when in the attempt to please you I betray myself.

Lacking in love to you, when I try to make you be the way I want you, instead of accepting you as you really are. You are you, I am me".

Fritz Perls

There is a set of emotions and actions that can help us identify if we are establishing toxic or nurturing relationships. In particular, we find an intrinsic relationship between a person's self-esteem and the way he relates to others.

TOXIC PEOPLE

◊ They make you feel exhausted after being with them, because they are a volcano of emotions.

◊ They often feel dissatisfied in their interpersonal relationships, due to lack of flexibility in the face of conflict. A situation that makes them lonely and isolated people.

◊ They have difficulty listening to the other and establishing empathy. They regularly have a negative attitude towards themselves and others.

◊ They assume disrespectful attitudes towards the integrity of other people.

◊ They are intolerant of a disagreement, so they are easily disturbed.

◊ They have frequent negative thoughts and focus on highlighting the bad in any situation.

NURTURING PEOPLE

◊ You feel good to be with them, because they bring something good to your life.

◊ They are empathetic and are not afraid to express what they think and want, because they communicate assertively.

◊ They are respectful and nurtured by others, which allows them to cultivate positive relationships and increase their mental and physical health.

◊ They are pleasant and seek environments conducive to communicating with others and thus feeling good about themselves.

◊ They always value and enjoy what they receive from others. In case their needs are not met, they look to fulfill them for themselves.

Their thinking is more flexible and they seek to be positive with themselves and with others.

The essence of the human being clearly shows us a duality, that is, a conflict between what we are and what we want to be: good and evil, hope or resignation, among others. We are undoubtedly light and shadow.

Deepak Chopra and Debbie Ford, in their book called *The Shadow Effect*, point out that human beings have been socially conditioned to fear their dark side, which generates uncertainty. Some authors argue that it is during the first years of life that our shadows develop.

Debbie Ford points out that these *shadows* occur before our logical thinking develops, before our minds can filter the messages we receive from our parents or the world at large. (Chopra, Ford, & Williamson, 2014).

These approaches lead us to reflect on the impact that these *shadows* can have on our lives, on the type of interpersonal relationships we establish and in general how we act in different situations.

"Shadow is one of our great gifts. Carl Jung called it the antagonist; it is our inner rival that reveals our weaknesses and sharpens our strengths. The shadow is not a problem that we must solve, nor an enemy that we must conquer, but rather a fertile field to cultivate". (Chopra, Ford, & Williamson).

"The human being when trying to avoid that shadow, does nothing more than flee from that part of ourselves, fleeing from the shadow intensifies its power, that is, it generates the shadow effect. However, if we recognize, confront and control it, that is, if we accept duality, we will be able to free ourselves from potentially harmful behaviors". (Chopra, Ford, & Williamson, 2012).

REFLECTION:

Could this have to do with the relationships we choose? When did we learn this? And how did it develop?

As I mentioned at the beginning, I was in that dilemma after having had a first separation.

Having lived under the framework of the family "should be" and the "you have to" was not very easy, and although I was very rebellious in adolescence, I always attached importance to school and professional aspects, having a good academic performance, having a good life, helping those who needed it, as well as seeking help and improvement. And besides trying to understand why it was so different between my brothers!

Imagine I am Pisces, I like the humanities, I am very intrapersonal and interpersonal as a whole, and here I am again in a toxic relationship, in the middle of this crossroads. Now I will have to get out of it and feel in the eye of the hurricane again! And it really scares and hurts.

According to author Ted Zeff, in his book Survival Guide for the Highly Sensitive Person, one of its distinguishing characteristics is its ability to feel more intensely. "They like to process things at an intense and deep level, they never stay on the surface".

On a certain occasion, someone told me about empathic people or *Highly Sensitive People* (later we will talk more about it), which led me to read several authors in particular *Judith Orloff*. It was then that I began to feel immersed like a fish in water.

GENEALOGY

I definitely had to follow my healing process from so many situations I experienced, I felt the need to Investigate more, work in my difficult areas and look for more references, that is, seek professional help to locate myself in reality and focus on stopping to continue having the same patterns in relationships, and of course, manage to stop inheriting them from the rest of the emotional family tree.

Undoubtedly, we are the product of our family history and analyzing where we come from and what behavior patterns or beliefs our emotional tree represents, it helps us to have knowledge about ourselves and to discover how the family unconscious interacts with the personal unconscious.

"When you get sick, instead of hating that evil, consider it your teacher".

Jodorowsky

The genealogy of emotions says that we are ancestrally generating patterns, and I want to get to the bottom of the matter, because I know that if I heal, little by little my descendants will heal It is very hopeful.

"The mind does not settle; it is there.
Its quality depends on how you use it".

Jodorowsy

"Waking up is not a thing. It is not a goal, it is not a concept. It is not something that is achieved. It is a metamorphosis. If the caterpillar thinks of the butterfly it is going to become, saying: "And then I will have wings and antennae," there will never be a butterfly. The caterpillar must accept its own disappearance in its transformation. When the wonderful butterfly takes wings, there is nothing left of the caterpillar".

Jodorowsky

"The Geneology of emotions involves an awareness that supposes the understanding of the elements of the past that have shaped us, as well as the beginning of a future impulse to which we shape ourselves. Individuals can have a positive and a negative view of their relatives; each family member becoming a double entity: one light and one dark. Two energy fields that instead of opposing each other are complementary".
(Jodorowsky & Costa, 2011).

CHAPTER 2
Why do I Relapse?

"I'm not what happened to me,
I am what I choose to become."
CARL GUSTAV JUNG

VULNERABILITY

Now I understand a little more where all my family background comes from, a lot of traditionalism, times of ancestral punishments, where duty to be prevails, the having to, the fear of not belonging to a group or not being accepted in the family environment, the fear of not being successful, for not being a university student, among many other fears.

In addition to this, everything becomes more complex when in an increasingly common family context, the responsibility of educating and guiding the children falls on a single person, either the father or the mother, which they usually are able to manage but in lonely situations.

In this scenario, I had to face fears, doubts and indecisions that led me to establish toxic relationships. On many occasions I began to *feel guilty* about what was happening in my environment. I think many of us have felt this way and yet we were unaware of the true origin of our problems.

Identifying how emotional genealogy helps us to clarify the origin of our actions, whether conscious or unconscious, is the first advance made to begin to understand.

And what will we do with this information?

It is precisely here where you begin to act using your free will, your willpower, and your courage in life, because it is when you can be strong and say no to things that no longer flow with you, to situations that hurt, or behaviors that are painful.

It is when you can tell yourself "stop" and say: I decide to get away from everything that

"Guilt is a feeling accompanied by emotions such as anguish, sadness, remorse, or frustration. It is the result of a set of negative thoughts, where your behavior is judged and you have the belief that there must be a consequence.

Guilt can develop as a denial of a reality".

"Bert Hellinger (2002). points out that when a person has personal guilt, it becomes a source of strength if it is recognized and admitted. As soon as the person admits her guilt, she no longer has feelings of guilt; These develop when someone tries to remove or deny their guilt. The person who admits her guilt, however, has strength. On the other hand, the person who burdens herself with, guilt and its consequences become weaker".

is wrong. The time comes when you realize everything that no longer serves you in life, because they are issues inherited from other people that we unconsciously perpetuate.

Despite realizing all this, sometimes, when we feel tired, we decide to change because we understand that those patterns no longer work. Then, right at this moment, just when you feel better, what do you think? Suddenly a person comes into your life who makes all your efforts in vain.

But how is that and why does it happen to us?

After reflecting and identifying some limiting beliefs and patterns of behavior, I thought that the same thing would not happen to me again, that they would not hurt me anymore and I told myself that I was going to move away from all toxic patterns, how is it possible that I allowed it to happen again?

So I went back to search for information that would allow me to answer these questions, which again focused me on the characteristics of *Highly Sensitive People (HSP).*

Tips for relating with *HSP.*

◊ Speak softly when you are with them. They are very good at listening to you, so they need you to listen to them too.

◊ Don't worry if they keep quiet, they just need a moment of peace. HSP are born with great abilities of observation.

◊ Be honest about how you feel & avoid complex discussions.

Surely you wonder how to face this sensitivity in a world full of stimuli?

Characteristics of highly sensitive people.

• *They are very sensitive to their environment and to the emotions of⁰ others.*

• *They absorb the energy that surrounds them, both positive and negative, and they are not aware of it.*

• *They can feel the emotions, energy and physical symptoms of others in their own body.*

• *Sensitivity allows them to see a world saturated with stimuli.*

They are intuitive, compassionate, creative, and develop a special spiritual connection (Orloff, 2018).

To answer this question, we found that there is a condition that characterizes *Highly Sensitive People or HSP*: *"vulnerability"*.

Furthermore, if we add to this condition the presence of a set of "masks" that we acquire in childhood, we find that it leads us towards greater vulnerability.

The expert on the subject *of vulnerability, Brené Brown*, points out that this is linked to the value of the imperfection of the human being and it is precisely there where the courage to face difficulties is found.

Today's society makes us feel that in order to excel we must show that we are happy and successful people; failure is related to not being competitive, creates a feeling of little worth, and becomes a source of frustration.

Feeling vulnerable can generate fear and shame in people of not being accepted by others. However, it is a quality that leads us to accept the imperfect of the human being and its potential for change.

EMOTIONAL VAMPIRES

Faced with my need to find answers and with my interest in reading, I found another fantastic book by *Judith Orloff,* entitled: *"Emotional Freedom"*, and I discovered that sometimes other types of beings burst into our lives and make us feel weak or they know precisely how to make us feel *vulnerable* or afraid to relate.

There are people who wear a very pleasant mask that hooks us, but in reality they remind us of family members who had that type of destructive behavior (which we project). and when they come into our lives, it turns out that they manipulate

"The word vulnerability is usually related to a condition of weakness, where a person can be easily attacked or hurt, either physically or emotionally". For Brené Brown, vulnerability is not weakness, since it places us in a state where we are able to relate the will to recognize and connect with our vulnerability, which determines the strength of our courage and the clarity of our purpose. *"Our fear and our disconnection determine the degree to which we protect ourselves from being vulnerable".* (Brown, 2016).

"Brené Brown is a renowned American sociologist who has specialized in the subject of vulnerability, courage and dignity".

Judith Orloff is a psychiatrist and author of the book: *"Emotional Freedom"*, where she talks about *"energy vampires"*, that being people who suck your vitality and lower your spirits to such a degree that everything you do afterwards is inexplicably full of clouds and bad moods. (Orloff, 2011).

our emotions or old wounds and we feel that all the work we had done was not productive or that we are falling into the same pattern... but it has nothing to do with it!

Although it is true that sometimes we get hooked, it is because we do not know how to differentiate these people whom Orloff names *emotional vampires*, who also navigate through life.

Let's learn a little about this category of people, who are capable of lowering our shield and making us feel that we are falling into unfavorable situations. To do this, it is best to know the definitions proposed by *Judith Orloff*, and take her advice. She identifies the most common vampires.

"The word narcissist has its origin in Greek mythology, alluding to the extreme vanity of Narcissus".

Narcissist: A *narcissistic* person is egotistical, that is, he likes to feel admired, so he becomes egocentric, because he wants to be the center of everyone's attention.

This type of emotional vampire can be charming, however they are dangerous because they "lack empathy and have a limited capacity for unconditional love" (Orloff, 2011, p. 165).

The victims: They are dependent, they do not take responsibility for their actions, blaming others for what happens. They tend to behave in a submissive way, but they absorb the positive energy of the other, appearing as a victim as if the whole world is against them.

The controller: He always believes that he is right, but without realizing it, he will make you do or feel what he wants. Their personality is obsessive, they are perfectionists, inflexible, taxing and manipulative.

The critic: This type of emotional vampire is used to making judgments or criticisms, but they focus on the flaws or faults in others. They tend to underestimate others in a malicious way, so their criticism tends to lower the self-esteem of the other person.

The separator: At first they are flattering people and they make you feel good, however, their intention is to destroy, because they are based on love and hate relationships. When the separator finds the vulnerable part of the other, he or she is usually cruel and manipulative, trying to control and this leads to despair.

EMOTIONAL FREEDOM

⬎Let's say that all these aspects that we have talked about; toxic people, HSP, vulnerability and emotional vampires, these are the internal part that does NOT allow us to BE.

Many times the strongest, most confident or people with the best self-esteem are not always so. Unfortunately, we also have a series of emotional issues that, although they originate externally, for example, in our family during the first years of life, they also lead us to the generation of scars inside our Psyche (mind). and that can be the cradle of what later we will call our survival masks for life, since as long as they are not destroyed and forgiven we cannot say that we are living, we are only trying to survive.

SOUL WOUNDS

If we could make a category of the main wounds that impact our way of life, I think one that I relate to the most is the one presented by Lise Bourbeau (2015), which is complemented by the concept of

Lise Bourbeau, Canadian author and founder of the School Listen to your Body, wrote the book "The five wounds of the soul that prevent you from being yourself". This book leads the reader to understand how fears arise in childhood and how they can be healed in adulthood.

Analyze the repetition of patterns and how we humans protect ourselves against pain using a series of masks.

Shadows and masks. In her theory, she raises the importance of the first years of childhood, which is the stage in which we acquire our first shadows and these intensify or diminish in the different stages of our life.

In the following table, the five main wounds of the soul, the mask and the fear with which they are related, as well as their main characteristics are presented, according her.

"What is a soul wound?

One of the definitions of wound refers to anything that afflicts or torments a person's health or state of being.

The word soul, derives from the Latin anima which means: air or breath. Hence, in philosophy and psychology the soul is considered an immaterial, spiritual element of human beings and a principle of life".

Wound: Rejection Mask: Elusive Fear: Panic	Has low self-esteem. He considers himself a misunderstood person and is easily isolated from the outside world. He is overwhelmed by fears and emotions. He seeks perfection, so in the face of his fear of rejection, he can become an obsessive person.
Wound: Abandonment Mask: Dependent Fear: Loneliness	Has difficulty making own decisions. Needs to feel supported by others and get their attention. His emotions are easily unsettled. Presents victim attitudes, is easily depressed and often acts dramatically to express emotions and feelings. He has difficulty ending his interpersonal relationships, because he avoids being alone.
Wound: Humiliation Mask: Masochistic Fear: Freedom	Seek spirituality by offering help to alleviate the suffering of others. His eagerness to serve and help others is above himself. Therefore, he limits his freedom, putting the needs of others before his own. He is afraid of being punished if he enjoys life, so he rejects impulses related to the senses. He humiliates himself, because he feels unworthy and guilty.

Wound: Betrayal Mask: Controller Fear: Dissociation, separation and being disowned	He or she seeks to demonstrate a strong personality, ability and to impose his or her will, to disguise his own vulnerability. He strives to be seen by others as a responsible person. Seeks to be special and important, through honors and titles, grabbing attention within a group. He lies easily to get out of a compromising situation, however, he does not bear being lied to. He is distrustful and demanding of others. As a leader, he demands that everything be done his way so he can be superior and important. He does not accept the unexpected, so he sticks to his plans strictly to achieve control. In his interpersonal relationships he is usually manipulative.
Wound: Rejection Mask: Elusive Fear: Panic	Has low self-esteem. He considers himself a misunderstood person and is easily isolated from the outside world. He is overwhelmed by fears and emotions. He seeks perfection, so in the face of his fear of rejection, he can become an obsessive person.
Wound: Abandonment Mask: Dependent Fear: Loneliness	Has difficulty making own decisions. Needs to feel supported by others and get their attention. His emotions are easily unsettled. Presents victim attitudes, is easily depressed and often acts dramatically to express emotions and feelings. He has difficulty ending his interpersonal relationships, because he avoids being alone.

"A wound of the soul represents a deep mark in the life of the human being, related to painful memories, emotions that live in the memory and that leave consequences that prevent reaching emotional freedom".

Wound: Humiliation Mask: Masochistic Fear: Freedom	Seek spirituality by offering help to alleviate the suffering of others. His eagerness to serve and help others is above himself. Therefore, he limits his freedom, putting the needs of others before his own. He is afraid of being punished if he enjoys life, so he rejects impulses related to the senses. He humiliates himself, because he feels unworthy and guilty.
Wound: Betrayal Mask: Controller Fear: Dissociation, separation and being disowned	He or she seeks to demonstrate a strong personality, ability and to impose his or her will, to disguise his own vulnerability. He strives to be seen by others as a responsible person. Seeks to be special and important, through honors and titles, grabbing attention within a group. He lies easily to get out of a compromising situation, however, he does not bear being lied to. He is distrustful and demanding of others. As a leader, he demands that everything be done his way so he can be superior and important. He does not accept the unexpected, so he sticks to his plans strictly to achieve control. In his interpersonal relationships he is usually manipulative.

Wound: Injustice Mask: Rigidity Fear: Coldness	He seeks to control himself to show others that he is perfect, dynamic and positive. He tries to hide his mood as much as possible.
	Although he wants everything to be perfect and fair, he tends to exaggerate a situation or event, even becoming unfair to others or to himself unconsciously.
	He controls his emotions, avoiding showing them to others, he appears cold and insensitive.
	He is a specialist in self-sabotage. He struggles, always seeks to improve his performance and does not respect his own limits.

CHAPTER 3
How did I Get to this Point?

The Shadow can reflect something
much bigger than it is
ROBLES 2020

This is getting complicated, despite everything I discovered there is so much more to know and this search for answers makes me understand, as time goes by, that everything has a simpler perspective. I will not give up.

In other words, if I were to look back at my life of years ago, right now, I would realize that studying all of this has contributed significantly to personal growth. We can say that if we have lived 30 years with our old and closed personality, and that, if until today, we were allowed to study all these subjects for a year or two, of course it would be a reward for the time and the effort.

It seems that there is a lot to know, but the learning, elaboration and assimilation time is much less than the accumulation of years in which we have lived sunk in a ship full of negative emotions and that finally it seems that the captain dared to rescue.

Taking into account what we have talked about in previous topics, I would like to revisit in more detail the concept of *Shadow and Mask* in more detail.

SHADOWS AND MASKS

What is the "*Shadow*" and how to deal with it?

When we hear the word "*Shadow*", we imagine a dark image that is projected on a surface. If we transfer this idea to our personality, we find that this shadow represents that dark part of our psyche, generally unconscious, where we can find hidden, in the depths of our being, the most primitive instincts of our personal history, but also of our history as humanity.

Human beings are the product of our evolutionary and collective history, that is, of

"Our shadow encourages us to act in ways we could never have imagined and to waste our vital energy on bad habits and repetitive behaviors. The shadow prevents us from fully expressing ourselves, being honest, and living authentically. The only way to free ourselves from potentially harmful behaviors is to accept this duality. If we are not able to recognize all that we are, the Shadow Effect will partially blind us". (Chopra, Ford, & Williamson, 2010).

"Carl Gustav Jung (1875-1961). was a Swiss psychologist and psychiatrist, who dedicated himself to the study of the human psyche, which encompasses all processes of the mind, both conscious and unconscious.

His concept of shadow is related to those unconscious aspects of the personality, generated by personal and collective history".

"Human nature includes a self-destructive aspect. When the Swiss psychologist Carl Jung raised the shadow archetype, he said that it creates a haze of illusion that surrounds the self. Caught in that haze, we evade our own darkness and increase the power that the shadow has over us". (Chopra, Ford, & Williamson, 2010, p. 20).

"Shadow effect. Although the usual thing is to repress our dark side, the truth is that fleeing from that shadow intensifies its power. Denying it implies more regrets. If we are not able to take responsibility and extract the wisdom that is hidden under the surface of our conscious mind, the shadow takes over, and instead of us controlling it, it is the shadow that ends up dominating us". (Chopra, Ford, & Williamson, 2010).

Factors involved in creating the shadow:
• *Keeping secrets about yourself and others.*
• *Harboring a sense of guilt and shame. Criticizing yourself and criticize others.*
• *The need to blame someone.*
• *Not taking into account your own shortcomings.*
• *Separating yourself from others.*

the particular historical moment and context. Normally, our dark side is expressed through frustrations, fears or insecurity, generated by the experience of life, but also as a product of the values and ideology imposed by society.

"Crises are great opportunities to become familiar with the shadow".

Carl Jung

However, the shadow has its opposite side called *"light"*. Learning to recognize our dark side allows us to face those shadows and decrease their intensity and also allows us to recognize our light.

"Our deepest fear is that we are enormously powerful. It is our light, not our darkness that scares us the most".

Marianne Wliamson

In the book: *"The Shadow Effect"* (Luz en la sombra"), by Deepak Chopra, Debbie Ford and Marianne Williamson, we can find that for these authors it is important to make known what they call *the shadow effect*.

The shadow is everything that we do not want to be, that causes us pain or conflict, makes us bring out the worst that we carry inside. But that is not the most serious, because we are the product of an education, where we have been programmed to meet the expectations of others, inheriting destructive patterns or that have sabotaged our best decisions.

All these shadows are stored in our unconscious and sometimes they are the main saboteurs of our happiness, and while many people seem to have a more or less stable and functional life, in reality they have gone through life wearing large masks to cover their *shadows*.

In moments of crisis, our shadows will resurface, many times they will manifest as a product of the wounds of the soul that Lise Bouvoir mentions, but they also express themselves through their own masks. Wounds, masks and fears coexist in the unconscious with our shadows, which also originate in the first years of life.

So, as we have mentioned, the accumulation of shadows and / or wounds obtained in our first years of life, adhere to our unconscious and thus we will develop more and more complicated masks.

The duality between good and evil is reflected in the dark side of human nature; for example: war, strife and conflict.

Violence is a shadow related to under-controlled instincts for destruction like the aggression between a couple or between members of a family.

On the other hand, addictions are a reflection of the shadow. The consumption of strange chemical substances destroys normal responses to pleasure and pain (Chopra, Ford, & Williamson, 2010).

THE COLLECTIVE UNCONSCIOUS

To understand the duality that makes up the human being, we will have to address what Carl Jung called the personal unconscious, however, there is another type of deeper unconscious that determines us as human beings: the *collective unconscious*, which is not generated from experiences individual, but is inherited from the culture to which we belong and even more, from the history of humanity.

• *Recognizing the factors that feed the shadow also allows us to reduce its power. Chopra, Ford, & Williamson, 2010*

"Duality is where we are now. The shadow has surrounded us with the mist of illusion. Our divided self is our main and most damaging illusion". (Chopra, Ford, & Williamson, 2010).

"Our dark side begins to choose for us, depriving us of our right to make conscious decisions, such as what we are going to eat today, how much money we are going to spend or what addiction we will succumb to". (Chopra, Ford, & Williamson, 2010).

"The collective unconscious is not individual, but universal, because it has contents and modes of behavior that are the same everywhere and in all individuals.

The collective unconscious is formed from the worldview of an era, generally under collective contents that are transmitted by generations". (Jung, 2003).

The *collective unconscious* is our cultural heritage, the result of our experience as a species, it is a type of social knowledge that we share. However, we are never fully aware of it. From it, an influence is established on all our experiences and behaviors, especially emotional ones, they are related to an external influence that determines our experiences and behavior.

"Depending on the historical epoch, individual experiences and social context, humanity is immersed in stages of collective light and shadow. This can be identified in any movement or social trend. For example, traditions, customs, beliefs, religious ideas that are inherited from generation to generation and can be both positive and negative". (González Hermoso, 2017).

THE COLLECTIVE SHADOW

It is important to understand this concept, since sometimes we do not realize the powerful impact that the Introjects (attitudes, ideas or beliefs). and paradigms of previous generations have in our current life.

"Defense mechanisms are means that we use unconsciously to face difficult situations, distorting, disguising or rejecting reality and thus reducing anxiety". (Chávez, 2002).

"The collective shadow is unconsciously incorporated into human beings and is related to negative situations that have led to social problems such as: discrimination, violence and destruction". (González Hermoso, 2017).

DEFENSE MECHANISMS

In order to know our Shadows we have to make a very deep internal journey.

In this inner search, we will discover that there is a set of defense mechanisms that act as saboteurs and sometimes help us avoid pain and we are unable to realize them. This is how our unconscious reacts to face the situations we live in.

It is important to identify these *defense mechanisms*, because that way we will understand how we react to various situations.

The following figures explain the function of each of the defense mechanisms.

Introjection

ME   OTHERS

"Introjection is a mechanism through which we adopt behaviors, patterns or norms, coming from abroad, mainly from the family". (Sarrió,2015).

In introjection there is an important influence from the outside in the way of thinking and acting, since the messages of other people affect our life.

Example: "All men are equal".

Projection

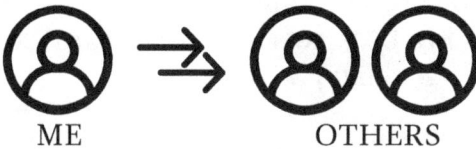

ME   OTHERS

"Projection is a mechanism that we use to defend ourselves against external threats, assigning responsibility for our actions or feelings to the others, (person or environment). The person places blames on others, instead of seeing that the responsibility falls on himself". (Psychology Madrid, 2019).

It is a way of avoidance, since everything I do I deposit or reflect on others and I do not assume my responsibility.

Example:
"I did not study because of my children".

Retroflection

ME   OTHERS

"Retroflection is a mechanism by which a person does to himself what he would like to do to others. In another mode, he does to himself what he would like others to do to him. The energy of action towards the medium turns towards itself". (Ugartemendia Maclean, 2019).

It means turning towards oneself. This mechanism makes a person do to himself what he would like to do to others. What we do to ourselves out of an unspoken desire, what we do to others but what we actually desire.

Example:
"I caress you, but I really want you to caress me. I caress myself when I need appreciation".

Confluence

"Confluence it is the act by means of which the borders or limits of the person are diluted and merges with the limits of the other or the environment or context where they interact. It makes a healthy rhythm of contact and withdrawal impossible and prevents true contact. It is done to seek acceptance and / or recognition and avoid taking responsibility for the action to be taken". (Ugartemendía Maclean, 2019).

ME   OTHERS

Acceptance of others is sought, where one's own personality hides, trying to correspond to the way of acting or feelings of others.

Examples:
"You are sad, I am sad".
"If my boss gets angry with my colleagues, I also get angry with them".

Deflection

"Deflection it is the act by which contact with experiences, feelings, demands, needs, both from the external and internal environment is prevented. It is the mechanism where there is the greatest evasion". (Ugartemendía Maclean, 2019).

ME   MYSELF / MY THINGS

It consists of minimizing the events that happen.

Example: "Tomorrow we see him, finally the boss is not there".

Denial

ME / MYSELF

It is the mechanism by which the subject blocks external events so that they are not part of consciousness and, therefore, treats obvious aspects of reality as if they did not exist. For example, a smoker who denies that smoking can cause serious health problems. By denying these harmful effects of tobacco, you can better tolerate your habit, naturalizing it.

https://psicologiaymente.com/psicologia/mecanismos-de-defensat

Denial. According to -Psychology&Mind.com-

It is the mechanism by which a person blocks external events so that they are not aware of consciousness and, therefore, they manage obvious aspects of reality as if they did not exist.

Example: a drinker who denies that alcohol abuse can cause serious health problems.

As its name indicates, the work of these *mechanisms* is to *defend our minds from the psycho-emotional impacts that we receive.*

However, once we understand how they work and especially their projection, we can take charge of our own conflicts, recognize what our darkest shadows are, forgive and ask for forgiveness for the damage caused and finally let go.

Once we manage to understand those shadows, it is more feasible that we can take off our masks and flow in life in a more integrated and congruent way.

Currently there are shadows related to physical abandonment, emotional abandonment, lack of security, low self-esteem and bullying.

> *"We all use projection to avoid looking inside, the shadow tells us not to look at our own weaknesses and to project them onto others to avoid feeling inferior".*
> *Deepak Chopra*

Denial signs. There are some signs that you or someone you know might be using denial as a defense mechanism. Some common signs:
* *"You refuse to talk about the problem.*
* *Find ways to justify their behavior.*
* *Blame other people or outside forces for causing the problem.*
* *Persists in a behavior despite negative consequences.*
* *Promise to address the issue in the future.*
* *You avoid thinking about the problem".*
https://www.verywellmind.com/denial-as-a-defense-mechanism-5114461

This is generally my case, but I think it is also reflected in the case of many of you. Therefore, I am going to take some time to talk about these aspects.

> *"It is ironic to discover that the courage to live an authentic life will be found in the dark corners of your less authentic Self".*
>
> *Debbie Ford*

Self-esteem

For the author *Walter Riso* (2013), there are four pillars that are intertwined with each other that make up general self-esteem.

📖 *For the author Walter Riso "Loving oneself is fundamental. There is no other way to take care of yourself and recognize yourself as worthy. Not only is it the point of reference for knowing how much to love others (...), but it also seems to act as a protective factor for psychological illnesses and an element that generates well-being and quality of life. If you don't love yourself, you don't know yourself as a human being". (Riso, 2013, p. 6).*

> *"When well structured, these four facets can be the solid and healthy self. However, malfunctioning they will be like the four horsemen of the apocalypse. If just one of the four elements is weak, it will be enough to make your self-esteem unstable. Furthermore, the opposite is true, if just one of the horses bolts, the remaining three will follow like a small herd out of control" (Riso, 2013).*

Self-concept. It allows us to answer the question: What do I think about myself?

Self-image. It consists of accepting and loving your image. How much do you like yourself?

Self-reinforcement. It is related to your own gratification, that is, it consists of analyzing to what extent you like yourself or reward yourself.

Self-efficacy. It relates to self-confidence, so it answers the question: how much do you trust yourself).

COURAGE

The age in which we live is characterized by a social tendency to lower people's self-esteem, either in face-to-face relationships or through the increasing use of social networks.

This trend is known by its term in English as Bullying, while in Spanish its equivalent is harassment. This occurs in face-to-face interpersonal relationships, while the term *Cyberbullying* is used for harassment generated through social networks.

More information on the types of Cyberbullying is in the Annex of this book.

In the *annex 1* you will find information related to this topic.

➘ Now, the time had come to face those Shadows caused by the issues that we have just explained, which influenced my personality, so much so that I came to present some very unpleasant symptoms, such as, for example: seeing that my relationships were turning very intense and unstable, my emotions changed rapidly and I had intense periods of sadness, irritability or anxiety. In fact, it sometimes became inappropriate and difficult to control these periods.

Chopra Ford & Williamson (2014), propose four steps to avoid the shadow effect:
1. Stop projecting.
2. Let go of all that holds you back.
3. Don't criticize yourself.
4. Rebuild your emotional body.

How to deal with the shadow effect? For this Chopra, Ford and Williamson, propose *four steps. From my own experience I add a fifth step: establish healthy Boundaries.*

Of course my self-esteem and self-image were impaired and sometimes I had the impression that others wanted to hurt me or injury me in some way. To make myself feel better, I sometimes took unnecessary risks like over spending, or overdoing it at parties, driving carelessly, or eating too much.

The author from this book –Courage to Heal– adds: Leticia Robles 2020.
5. Setting Boundaries and be assertive.

My mind returned to the memories and turned to an idea that at first had real bases, but later the feeling of abandonment of the people around me grew in my imagination, which gave me a great feeling of emptiness.

"What is a mask? It corresponds to wearing a mask that prevents us from being aware of the wounds that limit our ability to be happy. It is a way of avoiding and recognizing what has caused us pain, so fear is closely related.
That fear of reliving an unpleasant situation leads us to wear masks that only prevent us from achieving personal growth".

"Gestalt or psychology of form, focuses primarily on the study of perception. It studies the organizational processes of behavior and considers that a phenomenon as a whole is more than the simple sum of its components and experiences and behavior are organizational patterns. The "whole" is perceived before and the parts that compose it acquire meaning based on their "gestalt", that is, configuration". (Spanish Society of Psychiatry, 2009).

In this way, within my process, I have been able to realize *the masks* that I used to survive: being intellectual, the control, the codependency; which were formed in my first years of life.

Thanks to this I learned to stop feeling as if I belonged to a group of people that was not in "normality", a socially used term, but very subjective from my perception.

Later I realized that one of the dangers of being a *Highly Sensitive Person (HSP).* is that if we continue in life to be victims of aggression, bullying, intra or extra-family violence (physical, verbal or passive), or emotional trauma of various kinds or any of the five wounds of the soul -which we saw in chapter two-, perhaps we will fall into the risk of reaching the borders of mental health, including we could end up having some symptoms of Psychological instability.

Good fortune returned and I felt again the urgent need to ask for guidance.

Yes, I was one of those people who resisted seeking therapeutic help, much less from the clinical area of neuropsychology. Today I understand that I was wrong and needed professional support.

So, the easiest way I found to approach emotional healing was to study the specialty in *Gestalt Therapy* and years later neuropsychology.

I must thank many of the people around me for their support and my great teacher of life and *Gestalt*, and even so, I think that things opened up more strongly from when I started to be more formal in my process and in spirituality.

To understand this idea about the meaning of spirituality, I read another wonderful book entitled: *"Your Child, Your Mirror"* by Martha Alicia Chávez, which helped me clarify that religious and spiritual are not the same thing.

I learned that to achieve that spirituality we need to appreciate the beauty of nature, enjoy the manifestations of art such as music and all human creation. Meditation and prayer also become paths that lead to spirituality.

And so began the intense search towards RETURN TO ME with everything and the implications that this would entail.

If this habit of reading and searching in books has served any purpose, it was that another wonderful work by Debbie Ford entitled *"Courage"* came into my hands.

Debbie Ford speaks of courage, referring to the courage to face our ghosts, traumas and past hurts, which will allow us to heal our present.

Living with this value was for me a spearhead for the exit towards peace and personal balance.

When we lack confidence, we feel unworthy to have what we want, to speak our truth, to make radical changes that would transform the foundation of our future.

Debbie Ford's latest book, *"Courage"*, offers an alternative that allows us to have the courage we need to live the life that each of us deserves. As she says, "A warrior exists within you. It is there, but it has been ignored, repressed and has not been allowed to come to fruition". (Ford, 2012).

When we lose our courage, we end up in lives that are not ours, in marriages with people we do not recognize, jobs that do not bring out our natural talents, and situations that are toxic to us and the people around us.

"Spirituality is a fusion, a deep and real connection with the divine. With the superior being that is within us and that is in everything and everyone, whatever the name that each one gives to that Superior Being: God, Universe, Life..". (Chávez, 2002).

"Debbie Ford, coach, spiritual advisor and author, who in addition to having been an expert in the Shadow workshops, also did a work of introspection or an inner journey available to all readers with exercises, reflections and meditations".

Part 2
Life Lessons

CHAPTER 4
The Separation

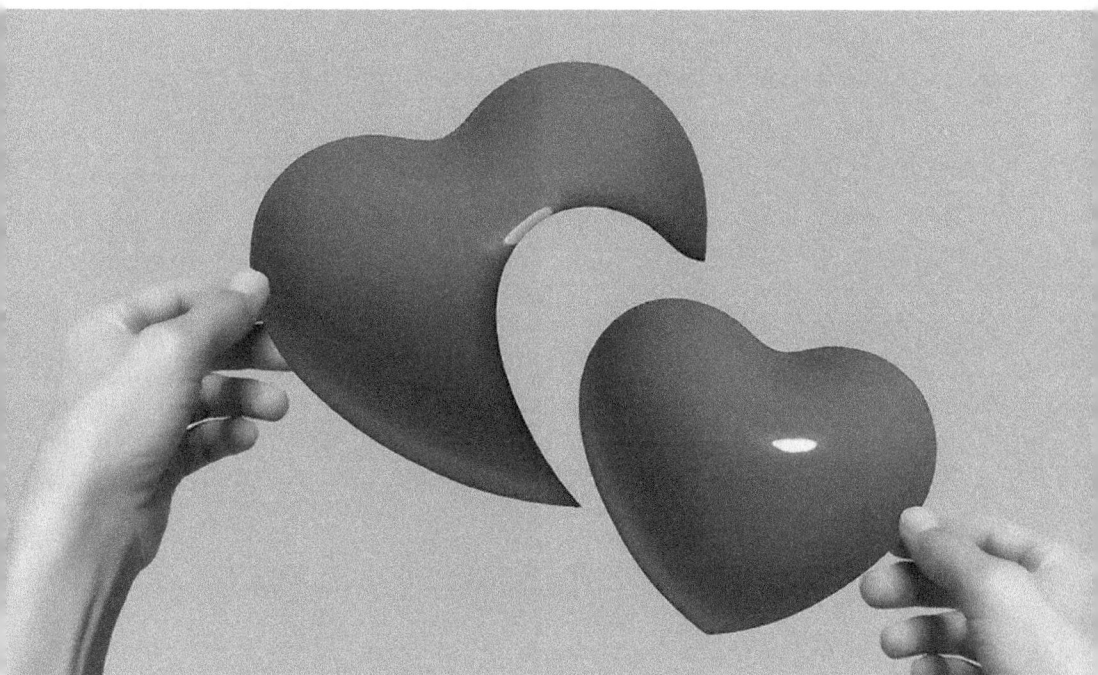

The first separation changes our lives.
but it teaches us to let go and to forgive.
ROBLES Y RAMÍREZ 2O2O

SURRENDER

The time has come to face my shadows, I could not continue to suffer in that way, nor make the people who loved me so tormented. It was a moment to defy the shadows, to dissect them in a serious and formal way, whatever it cost and whatever it hurt; To do this, I had to do something that was unthinkable for me years ago: I had to *surrender*.

The first step was to be aware of what I wanted to do with my life, but I want to tell you that it was not easy, one of the things I had to learn to do is to *let go*, but it was very difficult to do and let go of all the wounds of the past, a practice that I learned thanks to a book to which I will always be grateful for its existence, entitled, by Dr. Judith Orloff.

In this book it is mentioned that in order to make the leap forward, one must enter a phase of renunciation, and *surrender*; a term that is not equivalent to giving up, but a process that implies many things: realizing, knowing your vulnerability, facing situations, working through it all, and forgiving.

I believe that my codependency nested in the time that my complicated relationship lasted or perhaps it was from the times that I had to support my father to get ahead, especially emotionally, I don't know.

What I am sure of is that in this union the games of power and control, the lies, the abuse of time and other things, were terrible factors that influenced the relationship and that did not help the relationship survive more than a few years. Of course there was grief for the separation, it just wasn't that long a period.

"What is surrender? Surrender is being able to give yourself completely to something, in a flow that is in sync. It's letting it flow, listening to your inner voice about the direction the flow of life is taking you and making decisions in sync with that. Surrender can mean letting go of any previous ideas you have about who the "perfect person" might be.

Surrender is not failure, nor being defeated or weak, on the contrary, it is a strength that will help you face any contingency in life". (Orloff, The Ecstasy of Surrender 201

The relationship had worn out day by day, since several years ago; the continual disrespect and lack of appreciation led us finally to the lack of admiration that once existed.

THE SEPARATION

The fact is that when the separation came there was not so much to mourn because everything had already been cried about in advance.

Once reestablished from the negative behaviors manifested, with my self-esteem and my confidence raised, the next step was the most of my life after surrender, learning to *forgive and let go.*

It was the moment to say goodbye to this toxic relationship, -definition in chapter 1-, say goodbye, change my life and start a new path.

However, it was difficult to separate from my partner, although affection existed, my participation in the relationship was in great measure, codependent.

I discovered then that when possibility of a definitive break looms, our fears and insecurities become present with many doubts.

"What am I going to do in the future? Will I find love again? Will I be able to carry the burden of the house financially? If you have children: How will custody take place?".

In short, a series of *existential fears* arose.

It was time to cut with the past, lift anchors, free myself of the weight that no longer corresponded to me.

I was feeling much better, I had finished my specialization, I had taken several sessions

"Existential fears.

Refers to the search for answers to the meaning of our existence, lead us to seek answers in our relationships.

To face those fears, we create the illusion that some things will last forever. For example, we believe that our parents will be with us forever. This belief in continuous or eternal relationships guarantees us a certain stability at the beginning of life and then moves on to relationships". (Kingma, 2006).

of therapy: *Gestalt type, Cognitive Behavioral and Eriksonian.*

My life was beginning to take a course, I no longer felt confusion in my world of emotions and my catastrophic thoughts.

My joy returned, I began to take some classes of things that I liked, to go swimming more, going to wonderful natural places that gave me more meaning in life than spending my time on electronics.

After this separation I found myself raising my children as a single parent, with constant work that almost became an addiction, endless hours of work tasks, shopping, and unfinished business thus, my children grew up to a certain extent on their own while I ate guilt.

While we had a house assistant who helped with the food and the childcare in the afternoon, it was not the same as having had a closer relationship with them.

The question is that it was not the best for their childhood and adolescence, we had to go through very difficult times, for missing each other in the family, on occasions not being to share special events which caused great pain; finally the boys were growing up and orienting themselves towards their professional interests. Thus twelve years passed, extremely hard, sad, and difficult and with many challenges.

And so time went by, of course I continued with my healing process, although I encountered several bumps. stormy relationships kept popping up in my life, until I understood that many of them were related to codependency.

Cognitive behavioral therapy. The fundamental premise states that both our thoughts and behaviors impact on ourselves, but also on other people. "Therapy examines learned behaviors and negative thought patterns to transform them into positive ones". (Guerri, 2019).

Eriksonian Therapy. Milton H. Erickson, was the one who developed the so-called Ericksonian Hypnosis. "This is considered a type of self-hypnosis that favors connection with oneself and access to unconscious resources and abilities.

The purpose is that you can use them in consciousness in order to solve a problem". (Ruíz Mitjana, 2019).

CODEPENDENCY

The author Melody Beattle, defines a codependent person as: "Someone who has let the behavior of another affect him and who is obsessed with controlling that person's behavior". (Beattie, 2009, p. 16).

In the previous chapter, I commented on my main shadows and masks, one of them and the most important was the mask of *codependency.*

Codependency is the state in which our life revolves around others, we want to save them, take care of them, sometimes we feel like the victims, and other times, feeling powerless from the changes in the people we want to help, we become deeply obsessed with control.

In short, working through the process to leave codependency aside is extremely enriching, and although it takes time, it is a very important way to find inner peace. However, there are other things that sometimes get in our way to reach that status of peace, joy, gratitude and spirituality that we long for.

"Melody Beattie (2009). in her book: The New Codependency, makes a masterful definition of what current codependency is, whose most addictive substance is the emotions of others. It also explains several ways that will lead us to traverse the painful path that has to do with codependency: With them we can talk about the power to let go, forgive and start to stop controlling with our self-esteem and confidence".

We can do great work, achieve a therapeutic process, read good books and follow a process for change. However, we can achieve better results if we remember that we must work on the beliefs that we have buried in our unconscious.

Our beliefs can become limiting, because we cannot identify them. However, once our beliefs have been identified, once we understand them as limiting, what can we do? Can we change beliefs?

The answer is yes, since we can work on them, as well as we can decrease our codependent behavior, learning to establish healthy limits.

BOUNDARIES AND ASSERTIVENESS

"What is a Boundary? Boundaries are related to behavior, not the will of people, so limits have consequences". (Beattie, 2009).

Melody Beattie (2009). also raises the importance of setting limits in human relationships.

Setting limits allows us to increase our self-esteem, manage feelings and emotions, as well as learn to love, respect and value ourselves.

When a person begins to set *boundaries* in their relationships with others, a skill develops with which they feel more and more comfortable, because it facilitates establishing healthy relationships based on respect for oneself and the other.

When is the moment to set boundaries?

◊ If at any time you said what you really did not mean.

◊ When you identify that there is a lack of respect in your relationships.

◊ When you realize that you do things that you really did not want to do.

◊ When living with another person has become tense.

How does setting limits help us?

◊ Feelings of guilt and shame decrease.

◊ Change our belief about what we deserve.

◊ Our thoughts and relationships are clarified.

◊ They protect the most fragile parts of ourselves.

How can we set boundaries?

◊ Firm limits should be direct or specific.

◊ We must use a normal tone of voice, not shout and not get upset.

◊ It is necessary to specify the consequences of the acts.

◊ You have to avoid saying maybe, maybe, sometimes or I wish, I would wait, you should, I would...

◊ When there is annoyance or anger on either side, it is best to stop the discussion and try again at another time.

In order to establish limits, it is necessary to develop the ability to communicate assertively.

"The word assertiveness is derived from the Latin asserere, assertum, which means "to affirm". Thus, assertiveness means affirmation of one's own personality, self-confidence, self-esteem, poise, safe and efficient communication".

An assertive person is difficult to find, few people possess this quality: they respect others, express their feelings confidently and fluently, they are not tense, they accept mistakes, know how to argue without scolding while respecting others.

Assertiveness is the capacity to defend a point of view without leaving the other person in the background, without belittling them or making him feel less.

Assertive people are people who have all these skills, besides they know how to communicate in a precise manner, using a good tone of voice, with education and respect. And of course they self-control.

The lack of assertiveness occurs in people who have problems when it comes to relating.

In the real life, an assertive person has the following qualities:

◊ You feel free to express yourself in the most appropriate way and according to the situation. Communication becomes effective, clear and allows feedback.

◊ The assertive person has clear goals. You know where you are going and what you want to achieve.

◊ Knows that you cannot always win, but is not discouraged by failure. Reformulates, and develops a new direction.

◊ Establishes communication with a delicate style of speech, without offending the interlocutor.

CHAPTER 5
How have I Survived?

Life puts obstacles in our way, shakes us, throws us, but it also gives us
the option of transforming ourselves and starting over.
ROBLES AND RAMÍREZ 2020

THE ARRIVAL OF HOPE

A NOURISHING RELATIONSHIP

A few years later Hope arrived, who became a haven of peace, hope and love in my life. It should be mentioned that she was also a fun and very affectionate person. She had passed through a bad time because she had been widowed for a short time when we met.

In those years I only dedicated myself to teaching and working enough so that my children had a good education, a house and food and that was when we met in the summer of 2001.

It was a very beautiful time because the climate of the city –Barcelona– was at its best, and all nature invited you to go out and enjoy it. The walks through the parks, forests and lakes were long; the walks, talks and enjoying the people we met along the way.

They were days of tranquility and savoring the little things that life offered, of trips to many places and of great spaces to love... that... just love...

A quiet but passionate relationship, with many walks and coffees, but with a hint of sadness floating in the environment.

GRIEF

As I already commented, things got complicated in the end, but not for Hope but for me. I did not know what a mourning for the loss of a partner due to illness was,

much less if the loss had been sudden. Hope's ex-partner had died in a very short time of a rare disease, which caused much pain in the family.

"Barcelona is a Spanish City, which is located in a strategic geographical point, on the Mediterranean coast of the Iberian Peninsula. It is protected by the Collserola mountain range, delimited by two river deltas and surrounded by a prime natural location. This City has become a great European metropolis integrated into its surroundings". (Barcelona. cat, 2020).

Kingma, Daphne (2006), poses a grieving process that is based on the following statements:

- *I can't believe this is happening to me.*
- *You can't do this to me.*
- *I'm going to change, just tell me it's not true.*
- *It's my fault.*
- *It is your fault.*
- *I am no longer the same.*
- *The door of my heart is closed.*

His gaze in the morning sadly crossed the glass of her window and her beautiful emerald eyes were lost throughout her garden.

He drank from her cup of tea while he smoked a cigarette slowly and her mind was lost in the horizon... God knows what he was thinking.

At that time, I did not know the indicated time for people to go through their mourning stages, so I must wait patiently for it to elapse.

This journey can last from 1 to 2 years and in the case of not asking for professional help or better yet support from a *thanatologist*, especially when high codependency features are present, it could be lengthened and even convert to a pathological grief.

At that time, Hope's family slipped through long hours of everyday life and my arrival had been like a kind of slice of joy and new energy in the middle of the sad home, even where a wooden piece of furniture still stood in the middle of the house. with mirrors that contained the photograph and memories of the mourning ceremony.

Hope stayed there, day after day, every morning... motionless, staring...

The months went by... I went to his house, Hope came to mine in *Calella*... I came back... and noticed the same tired and sad scene again.

The furniture in the house, the objects, the house clothes, the dishes... everything remained the same as when the tragic event occurred.

I felt the gaze of his ex-partner from her photograph, strategically placed in a corner where it could be seen from the kitchen, the dining room and the hallway entrance. I literally felt with the company of her ghost. One night, I think I even felt her presence.

After several months of coming and going, with higher doses of depression, I gave up. My ego and my jealousy did not allow me to have the patience and prudence to take her by the hand and move forward, I could not cross that threshold.

THE SEPARATION

We had a strong estrangement, the separation came and I regretted it with my soul, because in those moments I did not realize that perhaps things would never be the same again.

This pain for the separation makes me remember the poem entitled: *Así fue*, by Luis Gonzaga Urbina:

"it was not a separation, but a tearing away"

Over the years our children grew up, and of course they inherited that tendency to stormy or codependent relationships from both. They all had a difficult adolescence with a hole in their hearts for lack of the other role in the family. Beautiful children, with good hearts, with good feelings... overwhelmed by their pain.

Hope and I kept remembering and seeing each other from time to time through the corridors of life, each one dealing with our own vicissitudes, always with heart in hand, always with hope.

Shortly after, momentous events arose in our lives and this would alienate us for several years. Hope asked me to rebuild my life because it was no condition to resume anything, as I was going through a time of great worry, pain and vulnerability.

THE TRAUMA

Almost 6 years after the separation I let go of this beautiful memory and now I –paradoxically– standing in my kitchen window, I wonder what

"Any separation, as mentioned by the author Kingma (2006), implies a grieving process, because it is also a loss. They live a stage of intense pain and face several stages such as: denial, sadness, anger, guilt, negotiation and acceptance".

"That's how it went Poem by Luis Gonzaga Urbinal (excerpt).

I felt it; it was not a separation, but a tearing away; the soul was stunned, and without any light, my thought fell asleep in the shadow...

(excerpt).

... my grief is very vulgar and you don't care.

I loved, I suffered, I enjoyed, I felt the divine breath of illusion and madness; I had the torch, fate put it out, and I sat down to mourn my misfortune in the shade of a tree on the road".

*translated by Sandy Hill

Cory Muscara, in his book: "Stop Missing your life", tells us with his words what trauma consists of: He defines it NOT as the experience itself, but how the experience impacted us. Two people can go through the same event and develop different levels of trauma, and what makes a traumatic experience is when our foresight, order and safety are compromised, combined with the inability to process and integrate that experience in a way that we cannot recover the flow of a normal life. (Muscara, 2019).

would have happened to the lives of our families if I had not had so much ego and he more patient.

They are those decisions that one will always carry the unknown in the soul...

That was the time to finish psychology and to understand the grieving processes, the truth is, I had to work on that loss a lot for several years.

As today Hope and I remain friends and we call each other often. We know that we will always count on each other.

But why is parting with a partner so painful? Daphne Kingma (2006), offers us an answer in her book *The Separation*:

"Since love is our protective shield, we want it to last forever and to be our absolute. That is why separating is so difficult". (Kingma, 2006, p. 13).

The truth is that when you love so much, there is a lot of nostalgia and melancholy, although some people also go through events so strong that they cause *trauma*.

TOWARDS NURISHING LOVE

After that relationship I set out to find more hopeful information about love, with authors like Arielle Ford, Ken Page and David Richo (among others). who were a wave of positivity and freshness at this stage.

In one of his online podcasts, *Ken Page* (2020). talks about the walls that we have created since we were little and that do not allow us to love:

Stage 1. Not being aware of the walls that we build ourselves.

Stage 2. The moment has come when you have to realize the walls.

Stage 3. Be aware of what has happened and view the wall compassionately.

Stage 4. We must look for a way to enrich our relationships, as well as find ways to articulate those personal needs and also to listen to the needs of the people we love.

And he also mentions: "Don't look for someone you care or like... look for *someone who makes you feel that your soul is safe*" (Page, 2020). and that's how my life was with Hope.

CHAPTER 6
Why do I Repeat History?

Our beliefs system guides us, but it is our decision to make them conscious and change the ones that prevent us from growing.
ROBLES AND RAMÍREZ 2020

BELIEF SYSTEMS

In short, working through the process to put codependency aside is extremely enriching, and although it takes time, it is a good option to find inner peace. However, there are things that exist that sometimes get in the way of us reaching that status of peace, joy, gratitude, and spirituality that we long for.

We can do a great job, go through a therapeutic process to achieve a change, and read good books. However, we will achieve better results if we work on the beliefs rooted in our unconscious.

These beliefs are those that we have kept in our collective unconscious and have to do with all the ideas that we acquire from our family and from the social groups that intervened in our upbringing or in the main impacts that we suffered during our life until before adulthood. We commented on this in chapter 1 and now we are going to break down the theme a little more.

Fléche and Olivier, in their book *"Beliefs and Therapy" (2014)*, mention that most of the time beliefs are unconscious.

Beliefs act as filters that guide our attention in certain aspects, therefore, they can limit our perceptions of the outside (*Flèche & Olivier*, 2014). When this happens, beliefs can be limiting and do not permit you to see reality with another look.

"Flèche and Olivier, in their book Beliefs and Therapy (2014), argue that our beliefs form a screen between the outside world, events and ourselves, beliefs perpetuate the sufferings of the past. So one of its main functions is to make our lived past go through time and repeat so as not to forget".

HOW ARE BELIEFS BUILT?

On occasions, beliefs are the product of personal perceptions that are internalized as thoughts, ideas or ways of understanding a reality.

Beliefs are not opinions about something, they involve three scopes: cognitive, emotional and behavioral. They are complex acts, which are distinguished from what is genetically inherited. Our beliefs determine our tastes, dislikes and our affective choices. Therefore, we can change our belief system, as long as we identify them and we are aware of them.

DECIPHERING BELIEFS

In my case, the beliefs revolved around some introjects that were lived in the family since I was little, for example, the idea that if you don't have a career you won't have a good income, that you are nobody if you don't study, that work comes first, that in life you have to be independent and brave, among others.

"As Flèche and Olivier (2014). explain, one of the operating strategies of the unconscious is to look for what is in common between two (or several). experiences, to proceed to elaborate a generalization that ends in the construction of a belief".

The last two introjects that I mentioned have been decisive in my life, however, dealing with others has not been easy, considering that I was a person more oriented towards the field of humanities and emotional and spiritual aspects than towards the systematic and scientific part (although I also have a side of it), and also considering that I was and am a HSP person.

So, when you decide to decode your beliefs, review their origin and work your emotional tree, you can look for the family origin of each of them from your ancestors (their struggles, aspirations, frustrations, their fears or the bases from which they arose).

Understanding that history or tree of emotions reconciles you with your ancestors and then you can change your belief system or modify them in a more positive way for your success in life.

For example, at the beginning it was difficult to relate my career with the humanistic part, since I had studies in teaching, psychology and a certification in brain health. I finally succeeded because these professions have bases of the scientific method, which is also closely linked to humanism.

EMOTIONAL DECODING

At the beginning of my studies, I felt as if I was going through a Stations of the Cross, since I compared myself to some members of my family tree who had achieved great incentives from their careers, without taking into account that over the years I too would have great satisfactions for my studies and experience, and that in the same way, it would put me on the path of writing.

For this reason, I invite you to take an internal journey through your emotional tree and that of your previous generations. It will help you find answers to the following questions: Who am I? Where do I come from? Why am I this way? In chapter 9 of this book, you will find some examples to go deeper about this topic, however, nothing is better than going directly to the reference sources that will help you familiarize yourself with this knowledge in a more detailed and enriching way, for example, *Enric Corbera or Alejandro Jodorovsky.*

In particular, I had an excellent experience in this field in the diploma course: *Self-knowledge, a tool for life,* by Pro-Eduk @, (Mexico, 2017), which was essential to understand my emotional and understand where my life patterns and beliefs originate from.

I have felt full of blessings

"Enric Corbera, is a Psychologist and Naturopath, who developed the Bioneuroemotion method, which promotes a holistic vision of well-being, considering that thoughts, emotions and beliefs influence our body and the environment.

Bioneuroemotion is based on scientific, philosophical and humanistic disciplines that study emotions and their relationship with beliefs, perception, the body and interpersonal relationships". (Enric Corbera Institute, 2020).

From before we are born, we begin to feel the emotions that our mother experiences and the acceptance or rejection of our father, through what she feels. We not only inherit our mother's emotional world, but also her reactions and feelings throughout the pregnancy.

Her joy and enthusiasm, her tenacity and perseverance, fear, anguish, rejection, guilt, all her experiences will mark our psyche, and from there in her womb our personality begins to be sculpted. The experiences of pain, fear or trust and joy will be important foundations and challenges in the future.

There is no perfect or emotion-free pregnancy, thus life takes charge of giving us enough material to work throughout our paths. Our personality is formed little by little with what we inherit from our ancestors, what our mom gives us in the first nine months of life, later the relationship we have or do not have with dad, later the way we react to the experiences that gives us life itself.

This is how our character (or prison), is forged and healing the wounds that lead us to suffering will be the door to freedom, learning and a legacy for our descendants. In the inheritance received from our parents and ancestors, there is a very important package that is the "family belief system". In that package go the potentials and gifts of our clan, as well as its hurts and limitations. In these emotional patterns and belief systems or ways of seeing the world, we have everything that makes sick and restricts us; the secret to healing is to transcend that information and make shine the pearls of wisdom that also go in the package.

At birth we bring in our baggage, both the glass through which we will see life and the tools to polish it. As children, we are silent witnesses and we obediently accept the dictates of our parents who with their words and gestures are shaping part of who we are. How mom looks at us, her words, the tone of her voice and the touch of her hands, her smell or perhaps her silence and indifference, her fatigue and everything we perceive about her, they are giving us the guideline of who we are for her.

Our mother looked at us the way her mother looked at her and she learned to look with her own gaze. The looks or the lack of them, their color, their intention, their warmth, their distance, their haste from generation to generation are recorded, until one day we see ourselves in the mirror, we find her look and we don't recognize ourselves.

Mom's and Dad's caresses give us security, their judgments and criticisms are the echo of their failures that will be recorded in our unconscious; their overprotection is our weakness, their trust our security, their abandonment our lack, their anger our fear, their cruelty our pain, their faith our strength, their joy our gratitude, their selfishness our misery, their generosity our abundance, their fear our terror.

In their great love, our parents bequeath us what they are, just as their parents did with them and from generation to generation, they leave us both illness and the opportunity to heal.

The mandates and beliefs of our family write the map of the route that we will follow when we start our way and until we have enough awareness to trace our own life path. The people who have given us this map are trustworthy in our childhood world, they have for us the absolute truth, experience and knowledge.

We will need to grow, not in size or in years, but in awareness and wisdom, to choose and experience our own path without feeling guilty for not following the path they have chosen for us and without blaming ourselves for what our parents chose.

Tracing our own paths and shortcuts requires responsibility and gratitude, responsibility for assuming our own risks and consequences of the decisions made and gratitude that without the route traced by our ancestors we would not be at the foot of this path, everything they have traveled in their lives serve as a starting point for making our decisions.

Mistakes are more than mistakes; they are the best way to learn on your own "that it wasn't there".

Although many of the mandates limit and condition us to see life with glasses that were not graduated for our eyes, they show us the look that our ancestors had of life, the way they knew the world and the route they used to solve their problems

Their experience is valid, especially when it is based on wisdom and respect, but maps with obsolete routes of treasures that are not real are also passed down from generation to generation. Awakening to the conscience helps us to validate, compare, weigh, thank, observe, analyze everything that we have been told about the path, our responsibility will be to discover and know the route that our feet follow.

The map they have given me has two pieces of information: terrain they had to step on and the way they traveled that terrain. In other words, it is the experiences they lived and the emotional states with which they faced them.

☆ MEDITATION TO REFLECT

This is my tree, this is my family, these are my ancestors. These are my roots, my past, my ties. Here are all the sins, the shadows and the darkness of my clan. The evil that I cause, the damage that I do to myself, the disease and the mandates that condition me.

This is my tree, my family, my history, my past, the lies, the secrets, the pain, the sins...

Tree of my life, I honor you and I honor myself, I love you and I love myself, I forgive you and I forgive myself. Sacred Divinity that inhabits me: Heals, renews, prunes, cleanses, purifies, transforms, liberates, protect, take care of my tree, my ancestors all take them in the Light of the Father, of the Source, of the Divinity.

Father, mother, grandparents, great-grandparents, great-great-grandparents, everyone. Born and unborn children, brothers and sisters, acquaintances and unrecognized, uncles, cousins, nephews, husband, wife, brothers-in-law, lovers, friends, my enemy.

They all live in me and I live in each one.

Sacred Divinity: heal in my tree what makes me sick. Renews, prunes, cleanses, purifies, transforms, liberates and protects.

Thank you I love you, thank you I love you, thank you I love you.

Part 3
The Exit Door

CHAPTER 7
Is There a Way Out of This?

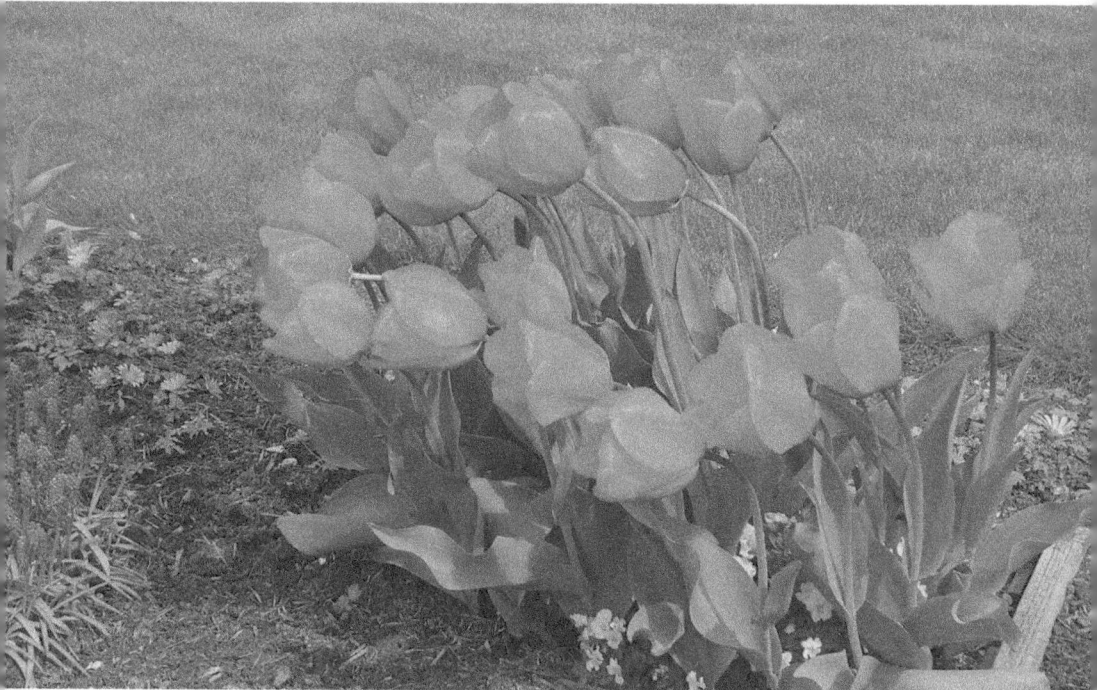

New beginnings... new endings.
New opportunities. great expectations.
ROBLES

DOMINIQUE

After a time of having healed and understood —although it took Hope—, I met someone who would become my new partner, also a foreigner, Dominique, whom I appreciated for her simplicity, solidarity, tolerance and positive attitude towards my children and with me. I don't know if I came to love her deeply, but it's worth considering that we were practically in the semi-silver years, and we both made an agreement in which we think that we could live together and be a happy, kind and respectful couple, with several projects and ideals in common, but above all we shared values.

NEW OPPORTUNITIES

This time I did my best to set boundaries on time and be a more assertive person. By then I had already studied several things that allowed me to have a better appreciation of the person who was my new partner. Finally, after a few years we decided to get married and this relationship lasted almost 12 years.

"Vernon is located in Okanagan, in the southern interior region of British Columbia, in Canada. The community is surrounded by three lakes and is known for its hot summers and mild winters, which has attracted businesses and residents from around the world". (Tourism Vernon, 2020).

Thus, with a stable partner, I soon found myself with my children immigrating to *Vernon*, where we stayed for several years.

We both tried hard to see what was best for the family however, fate played a bad trick on us: a disease occurred in the family that led us to lose most of our material assets and, consequently the emotional part that shielded us declined.

In Vernon we both had few job opportunities and soon had to return to *Calella*. Life in Calella became even more difficult, as there was a great economic recession, banks raised interest rates on real estate loans and credit cards. Salaries were low, income was low; We decided then to embark on the idea of starting a business. Bad decision. We were both we were quite trusting and they soon fooled us with the merchandise.

The providers were getting impatient with payments and it didn't take long for me to develop physical symptoms of great *stress* and began to consume food anxiously, which led to being overweight and later on to the growth of a *lipoma*. I had to undergo major surgery as my tumor was trying to break out through a hernia in my abdomen. Thus, a procedure that had to be carried out laparoscopically became conventional surgery.

The rehabilitation was very slow, the tissues did not heal, the drain hole took a longer time to close than the surgical opening. Healing supports were used, including *stem cell* implantation, and nothing worked. Also, a somewhat unpleasant mark remained on my skin.

More than ever I needed emotional decoding, since the diseases were recurring. I decided then to venture into the flower remedies of the English doctor Edward Bach (1886-1936), known as: *Bach flowers Remedies* —see chapter 9 Tools and resources. These solutions were very useful to me especially as emotional stabilizers, however, you had to understand the origin of the physical problems.

Even now, after 7 years, I feel pangs and tugging at the aforementioned scar. With my partner the physical and emotional distancing began; the problems increased and a great chasm was created. There were great silences, illnesses in both of us.

"Stress is a reaction of the body to a challenge or demand. In small episodes, stress can be positive, for example when it helps a person react to avoid danger. However, when stress is long-lasting, it can damage health. In a state of stress, the body reacts by releasing hormones. These hormones make the brain more alert, the muscles tighten, and the heart rate increases. Excess stress puts health at risk, including: obesity, depression, and anxiety". (MedlinePlus, 2020).

"A lipoma is a mass of fat cells in a thin, fibrous capsule that is usually found just under the skin. Lipomas are not cancerous". (Cigna, 2020).

"Stem cells have the potential to develop into many different types of cells in the body. They function as a repair system for the body..." (MedlinePlus, 2020).

The stress was killing everything. With my partner the physical and emotional distancing began; the Important things were allowed to pass for fear of arguments or a violent episode, sometimes emphasizing forgetfulness and lack of care for family belongings. We were even at risk of an accident, as Dominique was not adept at controlling cars while driving and I had developed *sleep apnea* as a result of the stress and pollution generated by the air conditioning.

This type of situation did not help to maintain the physical and emotional stability of the relationship so we were losing work and income.

Of course, I felt bad about the rejection, lack of passion, and lack of loving contact. Anyway, the family was surviving this new confrontation with the disease; however, there was not much to do, things were deteriorating rapidly. And it could be said that, although the feelings that united us in an intimate and passionate relationship were moving away, there was still friendship, solidarity and tolerance between the couple, which helped the family to function.

The children had already gone to study their career and we try to move forward everything that that economic loss implied, especially in financial collateral damage.

"Sleep apnea is a disorder where breathing stops or becomes very shallow when we are asleep. When sleep is interrupted at night, it is possible to feel drowsy during the day. People with sleep apnea are at increased risk of car accidents, accidents at work, and other medical problems". (MedlinePlus, 2020).

GRIEF SEPARATION

Either way, there was a dynamic of a certain functionality, there was camaraderie and friendship. Even so, surprisingly, my partner left *Calella*, without any apparent displeasure, a sentimental injury or a serious fault. Dominique announced it, without having given time to fix the financial issues, our emotional issues or stop going to therapeutic counseling.

Just as we were at the dock for her boarding the boat, I could see a gesture in those eyes that betrayed that there was not return. I remember that my partner asked for my blessing, I stopped for a few seconds, but I gave it, however, the body language indicated a final departure. I cannot express in writing how much pain it caused me.

The mourning for this separation lasted almost three years and during all that time I felt that I did not belong anywhere, because my heart was not prepared for any other relationship. Then another year passed of not feeling confident, of not having the confidence to move on. I had to ask for professional help to deal with the *depression* and the deep sorrow that I felt in my heart.

"Depression is a mental disorder, characterized by frequent episodes of sadness, loss of interest, feelings of guilt or lack of self-esteem, that impacts on the presence of sleep disorders, appetite sensation of tiredness and lack of concentration". (World Health Organization 2020).

Again I wondered: Why does the separation hurt so much? What is it that is so painful? This time, I didn't feel all the pain that I experienced in the first separation, but I had a dreadful feeling from losing someone I trusted would be my partner for the rest of my life.

My financial, emotional, spiritual and psychological security faltered and I didn't even know where to start or which way to go; the *depression* paralyzed me and the therapies and the medication were the only things that worked to make my heart begin to calm down. My whole body ached, I just wanted to sleep, I didn't know whether to wait, whether to hope, or how I was going to deal with the financial disaster left by the lack of another income.

SEPARATION TRAUMA AND ECONOMIC LOSS

Suddenly I felt that I had touched, once again, all the wounds of my soul: rejection, abandonment, injustice, humiliation and betrayal, because when you hide from a person that you are planning to leave, finally there is a betrayal of life to the pact of love that existed between them both.

It was then that I felt as if someone had stretched my heart, ripped it apart and pierced it. It is worth mentioning that along with this separation I lost all my material goods; but my heart recovered and my wonderful mind also; I came back to understand the *meaning of resilience.*

I still remember those difficult times and a tear does not stop leaking from my eyes, it was a terrible, long and pathological duel, after the first years, which were the most chaotic, I had to ask for legal help, try to reach an agreement of separation, however, it would take longer before having enough maturity for a divorce. On an emotional level, I was literally paralyzed for almost eight years. And now... what was next? How to start my life over? How do I get up and move on? It was then that I began to work much more on myself, to cope with that separation as worthily as possible and begin to draw up a new life project, thanking God that my children were independent.

Among other things, it helped me to attend self-help groups and learn to meditate. I started practicing yoga due to a terrible tsunami that life threw me:

In 2015, my dog died —adoration of my life— the business that we had started was closed

"The word resilience comes from the Latin word resilio or resilire, which means "to jump backwards". Therefore, resilience is the ability of human beings to face adversity, recover or get over difficult and unexpected situations. Being able to face difficult situations that arise in life implies a transformation in the way of adapting to changes, so it is also considered a skill that can be developed at any stage of the human being's life". (Psychoadapta. Center for Psychology, 2020).

(due to an abuse of some people who took advantage of the time that my illness lasted), so I had to start rebuilding my life in another way.

FORGIVE-FORGIVENESS

It is sad to admit that not even with all the information and the good heart that I already had, I still could not apply the verb forgive to this part of my life, although I no longer cried, as time went by I had to move on and start a new life project.

"Forgiving helps us leave the past behind us and to enjoy the here and now. It is the answer we need in our existence". (Casarjian 2012).

I started new studies, my grandchildren were born and even so it was very difficult to apply the word *forgiveness*. It is worth mentioning that I am talking about forgiveness as a verb, not a noun, not only as a word that comes out of the mouth, but truly feeling it. What saddened me the most was having lost my home, my trust, my security, my time, and not having returned to Vernon sooner to be reunited with my children; having had to pay so many debts, feeling immense abandonment and great loneliness...

SO WHY FORGIVE?

Forgiveness gives us the peace we want, it allows us to feel liberated from the attitudes of other people.

It relieves us of emotional turmoil and makes us feel better about life.

On the other hand, we find that forgiveness is NOT related to the following ideas: Justify negative actions, approve or defend behavior that causes suffering. Neither does it consist of pretending that everything is fine when you feel that it is not.

You do not need to communicate verbally or physically with the person to forgive. *Forgiveness implies a change of ideas and behavior.*

It is not necessary to say "I forgive you", although sometimes this can be part of forgiveness, because what is needed is to arrive at a change of perception.

RETURN TO SURRENDER

You cannot offer true forgiveness if anger and *resentment* is denied or ignored. The purpose of forgiveness is to free us from those feelings that are not beneficial to anyone.

When there is anger and resentment, these make forgiveness a challenge and at the same time a great opportunity for those who want to achieve inner peace.

Forgiveness allows us to change the perception of the other human being that we held during anger or resentment. It is a way of life that converts us, from victims of our circumstances to powerful creators of our reality.

Forgiving, therefore, gives us the possibility to love.

"The word resentment comes from re-feeling, that is, to feel again and again. It is a state of mind generated by the personal interpretation or the feeling that we have been victims of an unfair action and in which someone appears to be guilty for what happens to us. When there is resentment there is a predisposition to revenge". (International Federation of Professional Ontological Coaching, 2017).

CHAPTER 8
The Pandemic

Crisis are opportunities and blessings.
it is in your hands to take them or let them pass.
ROBLES AND RAMIREZ 2020

2020 A CRITICAL YEAR FOR THE EARTH

So, another 8 years passed, coming and going, creating grief, studying, writing, and healing my apnea —developed by brain toxicity issues— and thanks to this I studied Brain Health at *Amen Clinics, USA.*

Today I am almost completely healthy, reinforcing more and more my executive functions and in my personal work, which ultimately helped me understand my generational tree, and with pride, I can say that I am better and happier than ever.

In 2016 my dear father died, His personality was very controversial but who for some reason (or several). was my closest person to my family constellation. The road has been very difficult, but full of rewards.

My children decided to live in *Vernon* and my grandchildren were born there.

Now is the time for my children to walk their own paths, and to heal their own emotional trees; Let them pass through the corners of forgiveness and gratitude.

Time passed, and for medical reasons, my daughter had me return to *Vernon*, I said goodbye to *Calella* and packed my bags lightly and with joy, I left my *maelstrom* behind, I was filled with hope and I only looked to the future, I do not feel the urge to return more than once in a while to see my loved ones.

The birth of my grandson was a beautiful and an unforgettable experience, I was a young grandmother for the second time and those children have stolen my heart and brought

"Amen Clinics is an outpatient health care system that has provided mental wellness strategies to patients of all ages since 1989. It offers privileged experiences and personalized solutions for a variety of behavioral and psychiatric conditions". (Amen Clinics, 2020).

"Vernon is located in Okanagan, in the southern interior region of British Columbia, in Canada. The community is surrounded by three lakes and is known for its hot summers and mild winters, which has attracted businesses and residents from around the world". (Tourism Vernon, 2020).

"Maelstrom: Unbridled passion or mixture of very intense feelings". (Royal Spanish Academy, 2020).

"COVID 19 is the most recently discovered infectious disease caused by the coronavirus. Both this new virus and the disease it causes were unknown before the outbreak erupted in Wuhan, China, in December 2019. Currently, COVID 19 is a pandemic that affects many countries around the world". (World Health Organization 2020).

"Pandemic. An epidemic disease that spreads to many countries or that affects almost all individuals worldwide". (Royal Spanish Academy, 2020).

great joy after such dark years. My oldest granddaughter is a rainbow that draws smiles in my life.

In a few months, I received the news that Hope have had a stroke but thank God, has gradually recovered. We are still in contact and I am pleased to know that in some way I am useful to the family with my calls, and to improve their mood.

It's been a little while longer... as we are entering spring 2020, the news has been very disappointing since January, as a dangerous virus broke out for the third time in China. First it was SARS, then H1N1 and now *COVID-19* enters with force.

The word of its path through European countries is spreading and it is announced that it is becoming a *pandemic*, all plans are changing, uncertainty runs skin deep, fear does not wait, emergency measures begin in different places.

Then I had to make an important life decision.

I had to choose between staying in my home country... or reuniting with my family in the country where they chose to stay. They also wished me to return.

Despite the difficulty of the situation, I have learned that behind a great evil we can always find a greater good. My children moved quickly, and everything was arranged almost like magic so that once again we were reunited.

It has been a beautiful experience to count on their help and support, to see them grown, complete, making their lives happy; and for them it has also been very important to see me healthy, carrying out my projects, happy in this new stage of my life, being reborn over and over again.

Although with all these unexpected changes my work collapsed, as it has happened to thousands of people; for the time being we have found other ways to communicate with others.

The world is no longer the same, although separated, now we are together thanks to online strategies.

Being at home not only protects us from the *pandemic*, it allows our family ties to strengthen and grow. I no longer have to run from one place to another with the sessions, workshops and courses, now I can rest a little from so much pressure, I continue working and studying, with my heart full of gratitude in the peace and shelter of my family.

"With social distancing, uncertainty and confinement in our homes, you have the option of seeing it as a risk or an opportunity to reinvent yourself". (Moreira, 2020).

www.felipemoreiramentoring. com

A *pandemic* can be a tremendous threat or a field of opportunity, I could compare it to a war for the number of deaths, the economic collapse, the invasive and the terrifying... but I cannot help but see that I am at home, that I can help from a distance to those who need it, that this is an opportunity to trust and give thanks for my daily bread, just for today we are together, tomorrow will bring its own cares.

It's funny to think that now that I have less, I have much more, my inner peace, emotional health, my projects and above all the great love of my children and my grandchildren.

I know that the situation is difficult, there is great concern in society and the unbridled race of the media is also added, which, to sell more, release news that is half-truth and half lies, their media war to launch the most aggressive news and dramatic, as well as the power struggle of the different governments, cause enormous emotional instability.

But I also know that it is important to maintain peace and trust in life, that love and service are a great force capable of moving wills, there are more good people than bad in the world, and why not... those we believe " bad "also have the opportunity to find their light in them.

As the sages say, the darkest hours are just before the dawn.

"In a short time, videoconferencing has become a very useful tool both for holding business or other meetings and for providing online training through courses, webinars or online classes". (Classonlive, 2020).

And well... within the decision to stay in Vernon there are several variables, the temporary nostalgia of my friends... because it will take a little longer to travel to Calella again, the medical service that I will have, my clients from my work as a Brain Coach that I will work as remotely (via *video conference* to tailor courses for my students on an online platform).

RESILIENCE

I suppose that I will have to develop a new form of *resilience*, although, the truth is that I consider that all these years I have developed great strength in the face of the attacks that have occurred.

"KN95 masks are an important part of infection control in healthcare settings. The N95 designation indicates that the respirator filters at least 95% of airborne particles". (Centers for Disease Control and Prevention, 2020).

However, this is something unique and historical, thinking that we will not get sick with the *COVID-19* virus that has spread worldwide... we will have to face great challenges to avoid contagion: social isolation, the use of *KN95* or special cloth *masks*, the constant washing and disinfection of hands and products that are acquired outside the home in addition to the surfaces we touch on a daily basis... more serious: a brutal economic recession.

OTHER RESOURCES TO MOVE AHEAD

Anyway, in this situation I now find myself and looking for alternatives for inner peace, stress management and emotions, I found very efficient techniques from the *HeartMath* organization: www.heartmath.org, for those who might like to enter that Web site.

My findings at the *HeartMath* Institute were very important, I found a type of meditation focused on breathing in the heart, which has really been very good and helped me to lower stress and anguish and to obtain more resilience, I will explain it:

HeartMath Inner Balance Technique (2020):

1. Focus your attention on the area of the heart. Imagine that your breath flows in the center of your chest as if it were going in and out of your heart. Take slow, deep breaths (inhale and exhale for five seconds at a time).

2. With each breath, call forth the feeling of inner balance to equalize your mental and emotional energy.

3. Establish a true intention in the development of your projects or challenges, seeking an inner balance.

Internal Balance Technique: Applications

• Helps to discern about important issues, make decisions, or develop creative processes.
• Reduces the stress of the pressure related to time to do activities.

"Mission of the HeartMath Institute: Is to help people bring their physical, mental and emotional systems into balanced alignment with the intuitive guidance of their heart. This unfolds the path to become individuals with powers for the hearts who choose the path of love, which demonstrate through the compassionate care for the well-being of themselves, others and Planet Earth". (HeartMath Insitute, 2020).

"Vision HeartMath: It is leading to global change and people are feeling that it implies a deeper connection to their heart. This desire for more connection to the heart is a growing movement, to which people are drawn by a push from their own intuition or awareness to listen more to their hearts and connect with their inner guidance. The voice or feelings of the heart have been mentioned in writings and teachings throughout the millennia.

HeartMath exists to help individuals, organizations, and the global community incorporate the intelligence of the heart into their everyday experience of life". (HeartMath Insitute, 2020).

• Avoid frustration, anxiety or impatience with yourself or with the people with whom we interact.

So let's get to work, I have felt very well with the daily practice of this technique that helped me to recover my energy and also to send energy from the heart to all the people who are in the front line of the Corona Virus.

So, having learned that we have several human dimensions: that we are a physical, mental, spiritual, emotional body, etc., we forget that we can also develop our energy field.

In these days of confinement I have taken a course related to the Benefit of Resilience, where various *HeartMath* techniques were taught and of course also addressed the functioning of energy in our body, heart and brain.

They showed us that we have an internal battery, which can lower its energy level or raise it.

"From coherence, you feed your creativity and logical thinking while your body heals itself". (Felipe Moreira, 2020).

If we balance ours, then we can face things with a better perspective, more patience, less anxiety... become more resilient.

All this also led me to be able to extend this type of knowledge to other people from different places. Now with this vicissitude of the pandemic it has been very difficult to return to daily work, to be able to see clients or offer classes in person, so, for this reason, I concluded that it was important to be able to spread this type of tool to other people by all means possible.

www.felipemoreiramentoring. com

After taking this small course I decided to enter a worldwide network of Global Coherence called *Coherence Hotspot* (2020), where they offer you the tools so that you can form an energy balance point in your locality, this opportunity exists for all cities of the world, so when we meditate globally, we can connect with people from different countries such as Brazil, Argentina, Mexico, Canada, the United States, France, Germany, etc, to name a few.

This *Coherence Hotspot* movement is something very interesting and I recommend that if you are interested, you visit the page coherencehotspot.com so that you can learn about this type of training, in this particular site they have given me bases on: the coherence and the energy that the heart sends out and connects with the brain, breathing techniques that can control stress, anxiety and depression without the need for our body to enter chaos or have confrontational or traumatic therapies, of course if you have one of these syndromes acutely or chronically , yes it is important that at the same time these syndromes in an acute or chronic form, it is important that at the same time you have a psychological or psychiatric evaluation in your case.

These techniques have been very good for my development and to link them with all my therapeutic information.

Along with these contents, I was able to learn various topics from authors such as *Gregg Braden, Joe Dispenza and Bruce Lipton* —among others—, in addition to enjoying a great documentary called Wonderful World (subtitled in Spanish, from the BBC). that I really recommend you search for on YouTube, it is long, but it is very worth it, where the

"The idea for the global Coherence Hotspot network was born in 2018 in Bogotá, Colombia, when founder Dirk Terpstra worked with local communities and saw a great need and desire to heal the wounds of the past. The most effective way to do this is to open the heart and create coherence in every cell of the body.

Through science, innate wisdom, community, and awareness, we are currently making a critical shift on this planet, one that allows us to create a harmonious and coherent relationship with the natural world, with our inner selves, and with each other.

Today is the perfect time to get together, genuinely connect, and create a new future, based on connection, caring, kindness and compassion". (Terpstra, 2020).

"Gregg Braden... scientist, international educator and recognized as a pioneer in the emerging paradigm based on science, spirituality, social policy and human potential". (Gregg Braden, 2020).

"Dr. Joe received a B.S. from Evergreen State College and his doctorate in chiropractic from Life University, graduating with honors. His graduate training covered neurology, neuroscience, brain function and chemistry, cell biology, memory training, and aging and longevity". (Dr. Joe Dispenza, 2020).

"Bruce H. Lipton, PhD is an internationally recognized leader in bringing science and spirit together. Stem cell biologist, author of The Biology of Belief and winner of the 2009 Goi Peace Award, he has been a guest speaker on hundreds of television and radio programs, as well as a keynote presenter at national and international conferences". (Bruce Lipton, 2020).

"Edgar Mitchell: one of the astronauts who was a member of the Apollo 14 crew in 1973".

work of several organizations whose mission is to create global awareness is concentrated.

If we had known and used these tools for years, our personal, social and global awareness would be broader in order to prevent the spread of this pandemic and gather forces between countries, prevent issues of global warming and other types of situations, which this poor planet currently faces.

I also recommend you consult the *IONS.org* website. This organization was founded by *Dr. Edgar Mitchell*, who changed his perception of life according to what he could observe of planet Earth from space, in *IONS* you will find very good courses, conferences and many topics to be able to have a more coherent, ample vision of the world and a fuller life.

We do not know how this pandemic will end, we think we will be successful, unfortunately many people are going to die in addition to those who have already gone before us. However, today we know that, if we have a strong immune system, if our diet is good, if we consume the appropriate supplements and especially if we follow the advice of the Health Systems of each country, it is very possible that the infection will be much less virulent so let's get immunized. More education and solidarity are needed.

Taking care of our mental health is also key to coping with this situation, since acute stress and anxiety states, or panic, can lead us to carry out incoherent, ignorant, or risky actions to our health.

The organizational theories that I spoke about earlier help us to have a deeper and more human perspective of what life is like on planet Earth. A planet that by nature is abundant, balanced, rich in its flora and fauna, rich in its animal kingdom, and that we human beings have not been able to appreciate enough and dignify its value.

Mother Earth this time no longer allowed the abuse of the human being, so either we change our consciousness or we will begin to suffer the consequences of living in a disorganized, ignorant and worthless way.

There is no doubt that this is a great opportunity for human beings to reinvent themselves, to be more aware of their peers and their planet. This is a new age that will serve for the diverse human groups to transcend or become extinct; because the pandemic does not discriminate between races, creeds, politics, economics or education.

Therefore, I invite you, once and for all, we will continue to seek the value of *resilience and awareness.*

IONS: *"Science has profoundly changed the way we view reality, but there is much more waiting to be discovered. A more complete understanding of our world requires a more comprehensive set of advanced and practices. IONS uses scientific exploration and personal discovery to go beyond the current limits of human knowledge".* (IONS, 2020).

Mother Earth *"The Earth, perceived as a life-giving being, capable of conceiving and feeding her children, was seen by ancestral peoples as a female being, whom they called Mother Earth, because she is capable of offering the gift of life to the entire humanity through the fertility of the soil".* (More Sana Magazine, 2017).

CHAPTER 9
Support Tools and Techniques

A more creative, bold and holistic world.
ROBLES 2020

☆ BASES OF EMOTIONAL FREEDOM

We achieve emotional freedom when we are now able to give and receive more love, if we learn to work with our negative emotions instead of getting stuck in them, we will mature and grow in an integral way (body, mind and spirit). to be able to be great people.

As we saw in the decoding section, life will present us with various learning experiences: every achievement, every sorrow, every loss, every gain, every illness, etc.

Hopefully you begin to see your emotions, a vehicle for transformation (the word emotion comes from Latin and means to move).

The goal of emotional freedom is your conscious evolution, to increase your capacity to love and love yourself, it is your great opportunity to become a better human being.

Facing and working on your emotions is a challenge that requires courage, as we discussed in chapter 3, it is a truly transformative act, which will undoubtedly fill you with achievements, joys, the capacity for forgiveness and reconciliation with life. Do not give up.

When you are able to resolve conflicts, you will surely feel more alive and therefore happier. You will be a nicer person to yourself, your friends, relationships, and your family. You will be able to connect the power of the heart to overcome the most difficult situations, you will feel strengthened and protected by a spiritual force (Orloff, 2011).

Hunches you shouldn't ignore

When we make bad decisions that hurt us forever, we wish we had done things differently, we must avoid regret.

"Our initial hunch often hits the spot; however, we tend to reject it and instead rely on a practical mindset". Explains Dr. Judith Orloff (2011).

Being intuitive is something much more legitimate or true than an unknown feeling. Most of us have regretted some choices made in the past. A key cause of bad decisions is ignoring your intuition.

☆ HEALING THE PAIN OF THE PAST

Emotional release technique.

We begin the meditation with three conscious breaths: say to myself "I am going to take three deep and gentle conscious breaths: one... two... three" (the objective of saying this is to give a signal to the unconscious that means "get ready because here I go").

Next, we visualize ourselves perfectly dressed radiant, the best version of ourselves, standing in front of a very long corridor, everything is white and there are doors to the right and to the left, some doors are open and others are closed. (The corridor represents our unconscious, in the farthest doors are the most primitive memories, the open doors are related to painful memories that still hurt us and that we have not been able to overcome. The closed doors are situations that we do not remember, but they are there, wanting to emerge into the light).

Preferably I visualize myself dressed in very bright white.

I walk slowly looking at the different doors until I enter one that is almost at the bottom. It is an open door. I am going to enter a memory of which I have all the information, it is a memory where my father hit me, although it was not very hard, I remember his angry face telling me "clumsy, clumsy" I was very small, maybe I was 5 years old; this act generated a lot of fear in me, fear of being wrong in front of a male authority.

I stand in the doorway and see my surroundings. I see the dining room of my house, the furniture as I remember them and I see myself dressed in that blue dress.

I see the scene as I remember it, I try to pour myself water and throw the jug that falls to the ground and breaks, I see the father who approaches furious towards the little me and before that father hits the girl, I enter my current age but my best version, I stand in front of the father and turn my back on the girl (as a sign of protection), I tell that father all the damage he caused me, all the fear that that scream and those insults generated in me and they marked me throughout my life, I tell him that since that moment I have been afraid of men, their anger, their mockery, I feel insecure and fearful.

He cannot speak to me or touch me, he can only hear and see me and he needs to know everything I am going to tell him.

In the world of my mind I am going to tell that dad all the damage he caused that girl, I will tell him what I could never say either out of fear or out of respect or because she was very little.

I'm going to remove all the pain, the anger, the sadness, all the emotion that for years has been stored there infecting my wound. I will let the crying flow and I will clasp my hands feeling anger, feeling with my whole body everything I need to feel.

How do you know when to stop? Until I feel calmer, until the emotion subsides and my breathing returns to normal.

So now calm, I let the father go, I turn around and hug the little me with all my love.

I take my girl to a place where I remember that she was happy and felt safe, there I play with her and I give her all the love that I needed. I tell her what a wonderful human being she is and I tell her about all the good things that await her in her life and everything she needs to know to grow up healthy and safe feeling the deep love I feel for her, and she will also know that she will never be alone again.

To finish, I take her to that wonderful garden with soft grass, cool breeze and sun that warms but does not burn, I hug her tight, so strong that we become one Being: the little one will always be the joy of my heart and I will be the wisdom of his steps. To finish, I take her to that wonderful garden with soft grass, cool breeze and sun that warms but does not burn, *I hug her tight, so strong that we become one Being: the little one will always be the joy of my heart and I will be the wisdom of her steps.*

NOTE:

This is an example of how to do meditation, it is very powerful and with it you can heal the different stages of your life: your adolescent self, your self who failed in a business, the one who felt abandoned by his love; Any situation where the emotion has not been expressed, is just looking for the "door" and letting yourself be guided by your Soul.

We evoke the Higher Self, the best version of ourselves, to enter that great hall of life and open that door to help my most vulnerable, small, lonely and needy self.

In you is all the information to re-define these memories and turn them into healers.

When we refer to our parents of the past, we always think of "the father" and "the mother" it is not my father or my mother.

When we say the father or that father, we are referring to the memory we have of them in a particular situation, the memories are generally of the order of the childhood imagination, so we are not talking with our current parents but with the memory that continues to harm us.

In meditation we cannot touch that memory of the father or the mother, or hug them or ask for their forgiveness, the main objective of this exercise is not the father or the mother, it is you and your child, your inner child, that forgotten part of yourself that needs to be recovered, healed, protected and integrated into your life.

It is important that you can express and contact the emotion that stayed there, hurting, this is a cleansing and healing exercise and of course it will help in the relationship with our parents since we are removing everything that has interfered, everything unsaid.

Another very important point when doing the re-meaning of the memory, is the best version of us is observing the event, and since we already know the end, we are going to intervene before the aggression is consumed, we are going to intervene and protect the little one, Before being beaten, abused, mistreated, the little girl is going to look the aggressor in the eye, who cannot harm us but needs to listen to us and know that he did harm, not as an act of revenge on our part but as an awareness.

Trust that your Soul guides you and your protectors accompany you throughout the exercise.

☆ PERSONAL SWOT

Carrying out your personal *SWOT* is one of the best basic tools to move forward with your life project, look at the example and do yours at home.

SWOT analysis is a valuable tool applicable to various areas, including personal analysis, since it is aimed at obtaining a diagnosis from the identification of four factors: Strengths, Opportunities, Weaknesses and Threats.

Consider the evaluation of internal and external factors. The internal analysis involves identifying the strengths and weaknesses that you have, that is, skills, abilities, competencies or attitudes that characterize you, as well as the set of limitations or factors that you impose on yourself as a barrier to your personal growth.

On the other hand, external analysis consists of describing the opportunities and threats that exist in your life, so you should analyze your personal and social context, identifying those factors that can be the point of origin to promote or stop your personal development.

In a matrix like the one below, prepare your *SWOT* analysis.

	Strengths	Opportunities	
Internal Analysis	Identify the set of characteristics in which you stand out and that are important to achieve your goals and personal projects.	Establish the set of external aspects, trends or changes in your social environment, from which you can take a benefit and turn it into an advantage for your development.	**External Analysis**
	Weaknesses	**Threats**	
	Define the set of negative or weak aspects that you need to improve in order to develop on a personal, family or professional level.	Perceive those unfavorable aspects on the outside, they may be events or situations in your personal context, which prevent you from achieving your objectives, goals or plans.	

☆ LIFE COACHING

"Coaching is based on human development processes. Work with people regardless of their religious beliefs or personal philosophies. It is based on two motivating elements of people: self-improvement and self-realization (as it is written).

Life coaching is the art of facilitating the potential development of people to achieve coherent goals and in-depth changes. In this process, the Coach helps people to clarify their goals, whether personal or work, and to set out to achieve them".

In my particular case, studying life coaching gave me a broad vision of my opportunities 'and based on my weaknesses that I made in my personal SWOT, I was able to explore new options for my life project with triggering questions.

☆ LIFE PROJECT

Why do I need a life project to heal?

It would seem somewhat complicated to generate a life project to start a healing path, but part of emotional illness is not having a port to reach, navigating daily lost in the routine of living for living, waking up and doing the same thing with the same one again and again, not only with the same people but with the same thoughts, with the same problems and guilt, with the same emotions that drown us every day.

A life project can be as simple as waking up with gratitude, then sweeping with joy, bathing with pleasure, eating savoring, preparing food by blessing, going to work connected with the path.

I am the maker of my life, the creator, part of the problem is allowing my life to become a predictable broken record that repeats the same song over and over and jumps into the same paragraph. I complain about the same, I suffer from the same betrayal over and over again, I collapse before the same failure, I react the same to the same event day after day, month after month life after life.

I have the ability to sing a new song, project myself towards life each day in the way that I choose in order to reach the port of my bed satisfied for having lived with meaning one day at a time, with gratitude, enthusiasm or courage, breathing a new day every day.

Only by being aware moment by moment, and living present in the present, will we be awake to see the opportunities that life offers us and thus little by little we will expand this project towards the path that makes us happy, and it is as simple or as complicated as living looking up, senses awake with alert attention, writing our own script, dancing to our own music, not what someone else decided was the best for our lives. Living other people's projects only brings unhappiness.

Every night before going to sleep, visualize your next awakening, how would you like to wake up? What would you like for breakfast? How would you like to dress? And every day when you wake up breathe deeply, stretch your body, be grateful and prepare to live making the everyday, sacred, that is, doing a sacred act of the common things of each day, that your project is yourself, your life, your food, your breath, your walk, your enjoyment.

Although the storm threatens our boat, we are alive to face the storm, and no matter how dark the night is, there is always a ray of sunlight at dawn, your dawn.

☆ BRAIN HEALTH COACHING

Why do we need a Brain Health Coach?

This certification is achieved (among other institutions). in Amen University that depends on Amen Clinics in the U.S.A.

This certification help us to:
◊ "Specify the 9 Principles to Change Your Brain and Life
◊ Identify Brain-Behavior Systems: Functions, Problems, Solutions
◊ Analyze Subtypes of ADD, Anxiety, Depression, Obesity, Addiction and Aggression
◊ Describe how to construct Amen Clinics Method/Healing

in 4 Circles
◊ List Brain-Directed Supplements
◊ Identify Ways to Boost Brain Reserve
◊ Discuss the importance of Physical Exercise and how it impacts Brain Health
◊ Explain Nutrition/Gut-Brain Connections
◊ Examine the Science of Self-Control
◊Eliminate negative thoughts".   From Amen Clinics 2018

Those of us who have certified ourselves various Brain related questionnaires for evaluating and checking symptoms for children, adolescents and adults (anxiety, depression, dementia and much more). So you can find out how to use suggested nutrition, supplements, brain exercises, and lifestyle changes to improve your brain health.

This assessment will help your healing process to go smoother and a little faster.

☆ EMOTIONAL DECODING (Reflection).

Every map is stored in a Backpack... The two Backpacks

Your burden will be my burden. My freedom will be yours.

Let's imagine that at birth we have been given two backpacks, one is full of things and the other is almost empty.

The one that is full of things is called You Are and carries the heavy past, and the other, almost empty, is called *I Am*.

On the way we will need to leave the extra weight behind.

In a backpack we will keep the tools that help us on the trip; the other takes away our strength, it is full of: mandates, dogmas, fears, ancestral betrayals, allergies and everything that is "supposed" to help us survive.

The first backpack has the things that "The Others" put there to protect us; they gave us everything they thought we would need for our trip.

It is the survival backpack.

Each member of our clan gives us a gift as an inheritance,

something that was very valuable to them and that marked their life in some way, for better or for worse, the record of the event remained in the family unconscious.

The virtues, the talents, the predispositions to get sick, the vices, the skills are inherited, everything serves for our growth process, for our "awakening".

The diseases that we inherit also play an important role in our evolutionary process.

In the backpack that our ancestors prepared for us, there are things that we know and others that we do not know completely and we carry them out of an unconscious fidelity to the Clan.

In ancient times the worst punishment that a person could suffer was to be expelled from their Clan, this meant losing their identity, "dying" physically, emotionally and socially, losing their inheritance and even reaching misery and helplessness. To be disowned as a woman or to be banished as a man.

When the Patriarch tore his clothes, it indicated the worst offense against him and against the whole family as well as all those close to the Clan; out of solidarity and they were forced to reject the subject in question, otherwise this would mean a grievance and war between clans.

Living in exile meant being unknown, being erased from the books where the offspring was recorded, records that validated the origin, personal value and social position, being the son of, grandson of, great-grandson of...etc.etc.

Shaming the Clan was synonymous with losing one's life.

Many illnesses, failures and dire fates had (and still have). their roots in the curses and sins of our ancestors.

Loyalties to the Clan are engraved in our deepest unconscious and for our inner child, being faithful to their mandates, no matter how terrible they may seem, means: *Surviving.*

Our unconscious keeps memories of all our ancestors and

it is from this place of shadows and darkness that we move without realizing it and without being aware that we are walking blindly following the steps that our ancestors traced for us.

What is a virtue for you is a cause of death for me...

Each family clan has its codes, its rules, its secrets.

What may be considered normal in one family is a violation of unwritten family loyalty agreements in another.

If my ancestors survived on the basis of theft and deception, these are considered virtues, a family mandate: "Thief who steals from another thief, has a hundred years of forgiveness".

It would be very different from being a great-great-grandson of a man who stole and had his hand cut off for stealing and died destitute. The family mandate will be "You will not steal because misfortune will fall on your family"

On the other hand, in our family tree there are also those who place in our backpack rich sweets and chocolate bonbons, healthy and nutritious food, protein bars and some anti-acid that will help us on our emotional journey through this life: strength, kindness, faith, unconditional love, service, sense of humor, creativity...

Part of life is discovering that in the survival backpack you have, there are old things with the smell of musty past, a secret, the great-grandfather or great-great-grandmother put them there because they could not bear that weight and they left it hidden deep inside the backpack so that at some point one of his descendants brings it to the Light to be released.

In our backpack we find the silver chandelier (which generated discord between the brothers), the charcoal iron (which after so many years of use took away the joy of living from the aunt bending her back). the best silk suit of the cousin of Grandma (still new, always waiting for the special occasion to be released).

When we are ready, we will take out and release all that

weight of the past, only then can we find among the folds and hidden bags of the backpack the *pearls of wisdom* of our ancestors.

The other backpack is almost empty, there we are going to place all the valuable things that we find in the backpack of the past, which do not weigh and will help me while I am walking to discover who I am.

As we go into the deep path of our lives, we need to learn to let go, to detach ourselves from those burdens, from the beliefs that no matter how old they are clinging to the core of our existence. Imagine how difficult it will be to climb a steep hill bearing the resentment of the uncle for having lost his inheritance, the bitterness of the mother and her pain when discovering the infidelity of the father, carrying hatred and resentment weighs too much and there is no virtue that helps us to climb if we do not remove from the backpack this dead weight, which by death is taking our lives.

Now that we are waking up, now that we have decided to stop along the way and review what we carry on our backs, now that we have decided to leave behind useless suffering, we can clean this backpack of life so as not to pass on more shadows and bitterness, intolerance and submission ignorance and cruelty to the children of our children.

The others put a burden on their backs out of ignorance or inability to let go of their own pain and passed it on from generation to generation to reach our backs, but they also gave us many very valuable tools that are the ones that support our Tree, now it's up to us to heal to continue to flourish in our Eternal Destiny.

☆ A GRANDMOTHER'S LETTER: (APPLIES TO MEN OR WOMEN).

I found a very old map in the trunk of memories, it was the life map of my great-great-grandmother, it showed a path that led her to be ashamed of her body, to submit to being a woman enduring endless abuses first from her father and then from her husband. She walked this route until she hated her feminine forms in the depths of her unconscious, finding herself lost in the valley of tears, hatred, pain and disease.

On the back of this map it said in small letters: "I don't know what to do to change the route of my destination. God show me the way..".

In the same trunk was a beautiful parchment tied with a pink silk ribbon, it was a very old letter and it said this: If you follow this new path you will avoid repeating the history of the women of the family.

Accept and love your body. Bless your feminine being. Your beautiful breasts that show your delicacy and beauty as a woman, show your valuable feminine identity, the song of the goddess in your whole being. Forgive those who do not understand, feel sure of who you are and what you are worth, avoid the path of competition with men, hatred of your gender and their gender, devaluation for your body avoid cutting your breasts in sterile competition with the man, do not hide your beauty, do not feel ashamed because you are pure and beautiful.

Never allow yourself to be used, humiliated, mocked, abused by your being a woman, honor, respect and enjoy your body, do not poison it, do not intoxicate it, love it, so you will avoid losing yourself in the labyrinth of pain and disease, I already crossed that way, I lost myself for years in a grudge, stuck in the suffering of feeling like a victim. The path of forgiveness and love for yourself will be much shorter and you will find the route of your dreams by following your own path.

☆ *With all the love in my heart: Your grandmother*

MINDFULNESS: MEDITATION, BREATHING, HERE AND NOW, ACCEPTANCE

The word Mindfulness means *"Full attention"*.

It is the basic human capacity to be present in the present, that is, to constantly return with our mind to the here and now, to remember that life is lived from the present.

For 30 years this practice of Mindfulness has been integrating into Western medicine and psychology.

Being fully aware of our breathing oxygenating our body, feeling and connecting with each part of us, what we are perceiving with our senses, the land we walk on, the smells we breathe, the sensation of the clothes on our bodies, feeling our hair, the air that comes in and goes out, etc.

Practicing this type of meditation trains our mind to live in the present and stops the voracious thought that wants to live by anticipating and controlling everything. We stop ourselves from being addicted to nostalgia for the past and taking refuge in "all past times were better" "the sufferings of my poor life".

The continuous practice of Mindfulness is more than a training, it is a lifestyle. We learn to observe ourselves, to know ourselves, to obtain peace of mind, to enjoy everything that the present offers us at every moment and even more, ☆ develop a feeling and attitude before the life of deep gratitude.

GUIDED MEDITATIONS

Recover your values and honor your courage:

You are a unique Being, image and likeness of the Creator, of the Divinity, of the All.

Do not compare yourself with anyone, your Value is to be

Yourself, with your history, without judging your path, everything you have lived so far is what has shaped you, everything even the most horrendous mistake is part of your learning, of what that you are now, so recover your great value, your achievements are not small, they are yours, nothing more than yours, and they constitute the step of your own evolution.

Honor who you are that no one will do it for you, the courage to cry and acknowledge that you can't take it anymore, the courage to ask for help and make a stop in life, the courage to wake up day after day feeling you die, without energy and without reasons, the courage to continue living despite having no reason to do so, honor yourself and love yourself because you are here, looking for a way out. You are a unique Being, image and likeness of the Creator, of the Divinity, of the All.

Love your courage to wake up each day and continue to search for your own identity. Love and honor the courage to stumble and get up once again.

Close your eyes and take three deep and gentle conscious breaths, feel your lungs fill with life each time you inhale and release the load each time you exhale.

Imagine the best version of yourself, of yourself wearing your favorite color, you look wonderful, you look beautiful.

Feel the fresh grass under your feet, the sun that warms but does not burn, the breeze that refreshes but does not chill, imagine a large garden with the most beautiful flowers; nothing can harm you, everything is perfect, you breathe peace, you breathe love and recognition, you are the best version of you.

Hug yourself and speak to yourself with tenderness: I love and accept myself, I love and thank myself, I love and honor myself, I am the courage of my steps through this life, I am the courage to continue living, I am love and respect for me myself, I am the opportunity to create something new, I am Light and I am serenity.

Sacred Divinity that inhabits me, I honor you and I honor

myself, I love you and I love myself, Sacred Divinity that you inhabit in me I take power away from fear, I take away the power of criticism and judgment that has weighed on my shoulders, Sacred Divinity that you live in me, with each breath I regain my courage and honor my courage, so be it, so be it, so be it... this is done.

Repeat the three deep and gentle conscious breaths and gradually return to the here and now. Blessings.

Improving Your Relationships:

To improve any type of relationship, the most important relationship is with yourself, with yourself, as long as we treat ourselves badly, with harsh, critical, humiliating language, we will find relationships that treat us in the same way.

How would you like to be treated?

Well let's get started: Treat yourself as you would like to be treated and start treating yourself with all the love, respect and dignity that being yourself gives you. Look in the mirror and observe your image carefully.

How can you improve? Is your hair well treated? Are your face, your teeth clean? Do you treat your skin with love? When you see yourself in the mirror, what do you think of yourself, of yourself? Who do you see there behind that glass? Friend, friend, enemy of mine...

Your body is the house of your Soul, your body is a wonderful gift and it will accompany you all your life, how do you relate to your body, do you take care of it, feed it, caress it, make it thin, make it fat, subdue it, do you exhaust it, do you despise it?

Just as your body is the house of your soul, your shelter or your space is the home where you live, and you are the soul of that place.

How do you relate to your space, to your things?

Take everything out of your closet that is already old or broken or faded, keep 3 things that you like and you look good in, take out of your room what you do not need, put away things, clean, what you do for your room, for your space, you do it for yourself.

As it says in the scriptures: "Who is faithful in a little, is faithful in a lot" so to relate to life begins with yourself, with your body, your things, with a plant, with a pet.

If you interact in a toxic way with yourself, your relationships will only be a reflection of the way you love yourself, so get to work, you are the most important person in your life and as a result of the best treatment you have towards yourself, your relationships with the people in your life will improve, take out what intoxicates you and toxic relationships will also go away.

☆ Smile and value yourself and life will treat you with worth and give you a huge smile.

BACH FLOWERS REMEDIES

At the beginning of the 20th century, Doctor Edward Bach, a Welsh doctor, after a diagnosis of stomach cancer where he was given 3 months to live, left the conventional practice and turned to looking for a different way to heal the sick, something to take the patient as a human being and not as a machine that only had to be fixed in parts, taking into account that we are a whole.

In his quest he overcame cancer, he studied Hanneman's Organon (who is considered the Father of Homeopathy), and worked in a Homeopathic Hospital in England, until he abandoned everything to go into the study of medicinal plants and the personality patterns of people.

Why do we get sick? What do we get sick from? When do we get sick?

Coming to the conclusion that man becomes ill when there is a conflict between the Soul and the Personality, that the disease is not so much an enemy to be defeated but rather a messenger that communicates that we are failing.

Bach gave extreme importance to the role of emotions in

the process of becoming ill. Emotion is a powerful energy that, if not expressed or when it is exacerbated or repressed, makes the body sick.

His system consists of 12 flowers that work the personality patterns. Seven that work the chronic states and 19 in charge of the transitory states of the personality, as well as the states of crisis.

What are Bach Flowers?

They are remedies that are extracted from specific flowers found in the wild, from which concentrates are prepared from the mother tincture which later a personalized remedy is made for each patient.

Flower remedies are informational patterns, the flower has the pattern in balance and evens out the unfavorable pattern that makes the person sick; Emotions are neither good nor bad, as previously said, they are a necessary energy for the evolution of every human being.

For example, Fear:

Fear is an emotion necessary for the survival of man, on an instinctive level it acts as a protector.

Three behaviors or primary survival instincts can be activated: I paralyze so you don't see me, I run so you don't eat me, or I fight and face danger.

Nowadays, when we are no longer chased by a predator, but our unconscious (where our vulnerable child lives). interprets an event as a threat these 3 behaviors are activated. If when we were children we were terrified to read in public because the teacher (predator). scared us and his attitude was threatening, this act was imprinted; Already in adult life when having to read in public, one of these instinctual reactions is activated where reason cannot penetrate to take control, and we remain paralyzed without being able to say a word, at that moment we are prey to the terror that paralyzes; Emotion is out of balance, it disables us and plunges us into insecurity.

At the other extreme is the superhero syndrome and the lack of fear leads us to do reckless acts putting our physical integrity at risk.

The floral remedy acts by polarity, it helps the person who suffers a panic attack by introducing the pattern of information that balances the emotion, in this specific case the courage, the security but also, the structure and the self-care.

In therapeutic processes, Bach Flowers are great allies since the therapist opens the processes to access unconscious traumas and the floral remedy introduces the necessary pattern of information to balance the emotion that is torturing the patient.

Another example is obsessive thinking, that repetitive and recurring thought like a "broken record" that repeats the same song and jumps in the same paragraph over and over and over again. A thought based on misfortune, danger, bad luck, failure, fear, which, like a panic attack, paralyzes us, but in real life.

As collateral damage comes anguish, anxiety and insomnia, these types of

thoughts can be classified as toxic and destructive or junk thoughts. These types of trash thoughts lack sustenance and bases to be real, they are fed by fear of the future and by fantasy, we could say that they are torturing thoughts and only live in the heads of those who suffer from this condition and also, most of the time these people also suffer from misunderstanding by their family and social environment. The point is that it is beyond their will to control these thoughts.

In this case, the Floral Therapist will prepare a remedy with the information pattern of: Peace of mind, confidence in life, security, intuition, courage, transformation.

Floral Therapy has applications both in emotional disorders and physical illnesses, without detracting from any alternative or traditional treatment. In this new Global reality, it is important, from my point of view, to add, not subtract.

By working in a multidisciplinary way, with various therapeutic tools we bring great wealth to the integral health of the Person, helping to heal the body, mind and soul.

Floral therapy goes to the origin of the imbalance emotion.

The anger that petrifies the liver is softened with forgiveness, the hatred that bursts the heart with love is healed, the anguish that oppresses the throat, with truth is tamed, the acid critic that pierces the stomach is calmed with tolerance and empathy, the cruelty from the impatience that burns the soul fades with tenderness and prudence.

Flowers are the most beautiful, gentle and delicate expression of creation, it is a manifestation of Love, they resist rain, sun and the pounding of the wind, their value is hidden in their delicacy.

We could say that Flower Therapy are drops of Love that heal the Soul.

SEEK HELP IF YOU HAVE PROBLEMS OR NEED TO BALANCE YOURSELF AGAIN

It is true that today technology provides us with innumerable resources to embark on the path of self-help, but it is also true that when we are mired in the darkness of pain and suffering, we need a loving guide to take us by the hand and show us the way out.

The therapeutic accompaniment of the discipline we choose, like everything that has been presented in these lines, will provide us with the necessary tools to undertake the journey to our healing, no one can make the journey for us but in my personal experience, the best guide to leave hell is the one who has already passed through there, generally those of us who are dedicated to emotional health have lived experiences that have changed our lives and that is why we are here, as travel companions, on this great journey towards yourself.

CONCLUSIONS

Everything changes and passes from one form to another. Therefore, to find the courage to heal our wounds of the soul, you must bear in mind that you are a unique being, capable of renewing and rebuilding yourself day by day.

Matter, like spirit, is neither created nor destroyed, but evolves in transformative seasons: beginning, growth, peak, harvest, death, and renewal.

The possibilities are endless and limitless and that is what encourages our souls to continue and grow stronger.

You must bear in mind that nothing and no one is separate; everything is intrinsically and necessarily interconnected; nothing is ever complete or finished. The complexity of relationships of human relationships, based on the duality of being that characterizes us, leads us to constant and permanent introspection.

We are all in permanent evolution, assuming the new and letting go of the old, as we can adapt to the changing conditions of the environment, the challenge is to do so in the most conscious way possible.

"The past of things and people has a powerful influence on their present condition, but they do not have to be decisive for their future, it is in our hands to achieve change. Love, wisdom and healing endure as driving forces, both in our human stories and in the history of the universe". (Richo, 2013).

Reinvent yourself, visualize the infinity of alternatives that exist at this time. Understand the origin of your thoughts, beliefs or habits that limit your emotional freedom. You will understand that living is an act full of courage, where awareness and self-knowledge will lead you to live fully:

to live with **Courage to Heal.**

"Your vision will only clear when you can look into your own heart. Who looks outside, dreams; who looks inside, wakes up".
CARL G. JUNG

ANNEX

In chapter two we talked about highly sensitive, vulnerable people, different types of personalities like: The Narcissist, the Controller, the Separator, the Critic, and the Victim.

Harassment and mistreatment of vulnerable people have always existed, but there were no legal consequences as clear as there are now, at present this conduct is typified by the name of Bullying, becoming stronger and stronger and many times with fatal consequences for children and teenagers. The stalker has a mix of the first four characteristics mentioned at the beginning and explained in chapter two.

In Bullying and Cyberbullying, three parties intervene in the aggression circuit: The Stalker, the Victim and The Spectators.

The Stalker

The aggressor or stalker can generally present some type of psychopathology. Fundamentally, he or she presents an absence of empathy and some degree of cognitive distortion.

The lack of empathy explains their inability to put themselves in the place of the harassed and to be insensitive to their suffering.

In most cases, the aggressor has suffered aggressions due to an instance of power for him (dysfunctional family environment, abusive parents, belonging to an environment where the stronger abuses the weaker as a family system). The violent personality is gestated when the child is a constant victim of abuse and sees abuse as a form of survival. Constant abuse makes the person who harasses live with a feeling of repressed anger at the hostile environment, generating in him an impulsive character and a desire for revenge.

The person who harasses lacks social skills and tools for conflict resolution, he also presents a feeling of guilt that needs to be transferred to another, whom he considers "weak" as this person was at a certain moment, it is a form of unconscious "punishment" towards vulnerability.

The Victim

On the other hand, the victim is generally a person with low self-esteem, has a dependent personality, very attached to the family, generally comes from overprotective and dominant parents who prohibit expressions of violence, it is also the case in children who come from families where parents live on demand from work and there are few spaces for communication and coexistence.

The person who suffers bullying is generally unpopular, quiet and with few friends, these are very similar to him and are also the focus of ridicule, which hinders their social interactions.

It is common for the victim of bullying to belong to an ethnic minority, or to be bothered by a physical characteristic or a birth defect.

The "Spectators" or "Public".

In this circuit of violence an important part is the "spectator" or "public". The viewer silently or actively supports the bully, being an accomplice with his silence and becoming one with the bully.

The bystander observes the bullying, however, does not intervene to help the victim. Due to his personality characteristics, he feels strong next to the aggressor and does not want to identify with the weakness of the victim for fear of also becoming a victim. He amuses himself with aggressions, this makes him cowardly and cruel, reflecting his unconscious and repressed anger towards the victim and identifying with the aggressor.

The types of harassment are social exclusion, intimidation, threats, and most of this is accompanied by physical and emotional abuse.

There are several types of harassment:

Social blocking, social manipulation, social exclusion, intimidation and threats.

Another form of harassment is called cyberbullying, a term that refers to harassment generated in the field of new information and communication technologies, intentionally and repeatedly.

It is linked to the use and dissemination of personal or defamatory information through social networks, email or mobile telephones.

Some time ago we only had the type of harassment that we described previously, but what is unfortunate, is that although the advancement of the internet and social networks has supported us at work, with family and friend connections; it has also favored cyberbullying.

CyberBullying consists of these branches:

Online harassment
Use of electronic media such as internet, mobile telephony and online video games, mainly used to exercise psychological harassment between equals.

Denigration

Attack against the dignity of a person, using the injury or offense, through any electronic means.

Impersonation

Computer term that names the abuse committed through the use of communication technologies, characterized by fraudulently attempting to acquire confidential information.

CyberStalking

Monitoring via internet and constant investigation of information about a person or company. It is a premeditated, repetitive, obsessive act, and above all, unwanted.

Outing

Refers to posting someone else's private information.

Exclusion

Discard a person from a group or digital chat.

Sexting

Exchange, publication or dissemination of images with erotic or sexual content, generally produced by users.

Grooming

Harassment exercised towards a minor by an adult, in order to obtain erotic or sexual images or videos, without a relationship between both people in the real world.

These types of harassment can lead the victims to attempt to take their life, since they experience this torture day by day as a great suffering, they live it in solitude and in the midst of a feeling of helplessness.

BIBLIOGRAPHY & ONLINE RESOURCES:

Beattie, M. (2009). La nueva codependencia. Guía de apoyo para la generación de hoy. México: Grupo Editorial Patria.

Bourbeau, L. (2015). La sanación de las 5 heridas. España: Sirio.

Brown, B. (2016). El poder de ser vulnerable. ¿Qué te atreverías a hacer si el miedo no te paralizara? España: Urano.

Casarjian, R. (2012). Perdonar. Una decisión valiente que nos traerá la paz interior. México: Ediciones Urano.

Chávez, M. A. (2002). Tu hijo, tu espejo. México: Grijalbo.

Chopra, D., Ford, D., & Williamson, M. (2014). Luz en la sombra. Descubre el poder de tu lado oscuro. España: Urano.

Chopra, Ford, & Williamson. (2010). Luz en la sombra: Descubre el poder de tu lado oscuro. México: Urano.

Consejo General de Colegios Oficiales de Psicólogos. (2003). Papeles del Psicólogo. Psicología Clínica y Psiquiatría, 1-10.

Flèche, & Olivier. (2014). Creencias y terapia. México: Selector.

Ford, D. (2012). Courage. New York: Harper Collins.

González Hermoso, N. (2017). Cartas de Ética a un Estudiante de Bachillerato. México: Kindle Direct Publishing Amazon.

Hellinger, B. (2002). Órdenes del amor. Barcelona: Herder.

Jodorowsky, & Costa. (2011). Metagenealogía. Buenos Aires: Sudamericana.

Jung, C. (2003). Arquetipos e inconsciente colectivo. Barcelona: Paidós.

Kingma, D. R. (2006). La separación. Buenos Aires, Argentina: Grupo Editorial Lumen.

Moreira, F. (05 de 2020). Curso Resiliencia del Corazón. México.

Muscara, C. (2019). Stop missing your life. Lifelong Books.

Orloff, J. (2011). Libertad emocional. Cómo dejar de ser víctima de las emociones negativas. Barcelona: Obelisco.

Orloff, J. (2016). El éxtasis de fluir. Barcelona: Ediciones obelisco.

Orloff, J. (2018). Guía de supervivencia para personas altamente empáticas y sensibles. Sirio.

Paz, O. (1957). Piedra del sol.

Perls, F. (1974). Sueños y existencia. Terapia gestáltica. Chile: Cuatro vientos.

Richo, D. (2013). Las cinco cosas que no podemos cambiar. México: Alfaomega.

Riso, W. (2013). Guía Práctica para Mejorar la Autoestima. México: Phronesis.

Sociedad Española de Psiquiatría. (2009). Manual del residente en Psiquiatría. Madrid: ENE Life Publicidad S.A y Editores.

Stamateas, B. (2012). Emociones tóxicas. Barcelona: Ediciones B, S. A.

Terpstra, D. (2020).

Zeff, T. (2018). La guía para las personas altamente sensibles: Habilidades esenciales para vivir en un mundo sobresaturado de estímulos. España: Urano.

Alzheimer´s Association. (2020). Alz.org. Obtenido de https://www.alz. org/alzheimer-demencia/que-es-la-enfermedad-de-alzheimer

Amenclinics. (06 de 2020). Obtenido de https://www.amenclinics.com/ https://www.amenclinics.com/conditions/oppositional-defiant-disorder/

BBC News. (24 de febrero de 2017). Obtenido de https://www.bbc.com/ mundo/noticias

Barcelona.cat. (06 de 2020). Obtenido de https://meet.barcelona.cat/es/

Bruce Lipton. (06 de 2020). Obtenido de https://www.brucelipton.com/

Centros para el control y prevención de enfermedades. (06 de 2020). Obtenido de https://www.cdc.gov/spanish/niosh/docs/2013-138_sp/ default.html

Cigna. (06 de 2020). Obtenido de https://www.cigna.com/individuals-families/health-wellness/hw-en-espanol/temas-de-salud/lipoma-tm6295spec

Classonlive. (06 de 2020). Obtenido de https://www.classonlive.com/ blog/20-programas-para-hacer-videoconferencia

Clínica Dávila. (06 de 2020). Obtenido de https://www.davila.cl/hernias-de-la-pared-abdominal-que-son-y-por-que-se-producen/

Coherence Hotspot. (2020). Obtenido de https://www.coherencehotspot.com/

Dr. Joe Dispenza. (06 de 2020). Obtenido de https://drjoedispenza.com/ pages/about

EcuRed. (23 de enero de 2020). Obtenido de https://www.ecured.cu/ Alejandro_Jodorowsky#Psicomagia_y_psicogenealog.C3.ADa

Enric Corbera Institute. (2020). Enric Corbera Institute. Aprender a desaprender. Obtenido de https://www.enriccorberainstitute.com/

Federación Internacional de Coaching Ontológico Profesional . (2017). FICOP. Obtenido de El mundo de las emociones: https://www.ficop.org/bibliotecaficop/151-el-mundo-de-las-emociones

Felipe Moreira. (2020). Obtenido de Desarrollo de Inteligencia Emocional, Liderazgo y Administración del estrés: http://www.felipemoreiramentoring.com/

Gregg Braden. (06 de 2020). Obtenido de https://www.greggbraden.com/

Guerri, M. (2019). Psicoactiva. Obtenido de La terapia cognitivo conductual: https://www.psicoactiva.com/blog/la-terapia-cognitivo-conductual/

He Institute, H. (19 de mayo de 2020). HeartMarth Institute. Obtenido de https://www.heartmath.org/

Instituto Mexicano de Tanatología. (14 de marzo de 2020). Obtenido de http://tanatologia.org.mx/que-es-tanatologia/

artMath Insitute. (23 de Enero de 2020). Obtenido de https://www.heartmath.org/

Hellinger Sciencia. (2019). Obtenido de Constelaciones familiares: https://www.hellinger.com/es/home/constelaciones-familiares-hellingerr/

IONS. (06 de 2020). Obtenido de https://noetic.org/

Mediline Plus. (2020). Obtenido de https://medlineplus.gov/

MedlinePlus. (06 de 2020). Obtenido de https://medlineplus.gov/spanish/ency/article/003211.htm

MedlinePlus. (06 de 2020). Obtenido de https://medlineplus.gov/spanish/stemcells.html

MedlinePlus. (06 de 2020). Obtenido de https://medlineplus.gov/spanish/sleepapnea.html

Organización Mundial de la Salud. (2020). Obtenido de https://www.who.int/topics/depression/es/

Organización Mundial de la Salud. (06 de 2020). Obtenido de https://www.who.int/es/emergencies/diseases/novel-coronavirus-2019/advice-for-public/q-a-coronaviruses

Orgnización Mundial de la Salud. (05 de 2020). Obtenido de https://www.who.int/es/emergencies/diseases/novel-coronavirus-2019/advice-for-public/q-a-coronaviruses

Page, K. (18 de 4 de 2020). *The deeper dating podcast.* Obtenido de https://deeperdatingpodcast.com/

Portal oficial de turismo de España. (06 de 2020). Obtenido de https://www.spain.info/es/destino/calella/

Psicoadapta. Centro de Psicología. (2020). Obtenido de https://www.psicoadapta.es/

Psicologia y Mente https://psicologiaymente.com/psicologia/mecanismos-de-defensa

Psicología Madrid. (26 de Marzo de 2019). Obtenido de Los mecanismos de defensa: www.psicologiamadrid.es/articulos/salud

Real Academia Española. (05 de 2020). Obtenido de https://dle.rae.es/vor%C3%A1gine

Revista Electrónica de Portales Médicos. (06 de 2020). Obtenido de https://www.revista-portalesmedicos.com/revista-medica/drenajes-cirugia-tipos-cuidados-de-enfermeria/

Revista Más Sana. (05 de 2017). Obtenido de https://massanarevista.com/2017/05/03/por-que-llamamos-madre-a-la-tierra/

Ruíz Mitjana, L. (2019). *Psicología y Mente.* Obtenido de Hipnosis Ericksoniana: qué es y cómo se usa en terapia: https://psicologiaymente.com/clinica/hipnosis-ericksoniana

Sarrió, C. (26 de noviembre de 2015). *Terapia Gestalt Valencia.* Obtenido de Fases del proceso de contacto. Perls y Goodman: https://www.gestalt-terapia.es/fases-del-proceso-de-contacto-gestalt/

Tourism Vernon. (06 de 2020). Obtenido de https://www.tourismvernon.com/en/discover/City-of-Vernon.aspx

Ugartemendía Maclean, L. (26 de Septiembre de 2019). *Gestaltnet.* Obtenido de Estudio de mecanismos de bloque en personas con rosácea: https://gestaltnet.net/gestaltoteca/documentos/tesinas-tesis-doctorales/

Very Well Mind. The Denial

https://www.verywellmind.com/denial-as-a-defense-mechanism-5114461

Authors Contact Details

BHCC. Leticia Robles García

Certified Brain Health Coach

Integrative therapies

https://letyroblesavefenix.wixsite.com/letywriterandcoach

https://www.amazon.com/Irma-Leticia-Robles-Garcia/e/

letyrobles.avefenix@gmail.com

Mtra. Norma González Hermoso

Masters in Education

Director Ave Fénix

https://www.amazon.com/Norma-González-Hermoso/e/

https://www.facebook.com/NormaHermosoEscritora/

hermoso.avefenix@gmail.com

Mtra. María del Rocío Vázquez Escalona

Maester in Advanced Bach Flowers, Holistic Therapist

Expert in therapy with visuospatial children and adults

rociovazqueze@gmail.com

+56 1509.9361

About the Authors

Irma Leticia Robles García

She is a Teacher, a Certified Brain Health Coach and writer. Currently, she works as a Consultant and Coach in Integrative Health, teaches face-to-face and online courses on topics of Self-publication, Psychology, Evolutionary Awareness and Resilience in the 21st century.

She has published several books in a Conventional Publisher in México, and now with Amazon and Balboa Press.

https://letyroblesavefenix.wixsite.com/letywriterandcoach

Norma González Hermoso

She obtained a Bachelor's degree in Pedagogy from the National Autonomous University of Mexico (UNAM), with a Specialty in Higher Secondary Education Teaching Competencies, and a Master's Degree in Education with Intervention in Educational Practice.

She is also an advisor on research and innovation projects and technological prototypes, as well as an instructor in both face-to-face and online teacher training courses.

She is the author of the book: Ethics Letters to a High School student.

María del Rocío Vázquez Escalona

Maester in Therapy in Floral Systems and Psychopathology, Emotional Body Reading, has a Certification in Visual spatial Learning, as well as in the study of Ancestrology and Bioneuroemotion topics.

She is a speaker at international congresses of flower therapists. She is the author of the book: Learning Disabilities: A Monster with a Thousand Heads.

CPSIA information can be obtained
at www.ICGtesting.com
Printed in the USA
LVHW031114140622
721220LV00002B/272

9 781982 268572